A YEAR UNDER SHARIA LAW:

Memoir of an American Couple Living and Working in Saudi Arabia

By
Alex & Elizabeth Fletcher

Alex and Liz Fletcher

To Chantilly Lace,
You are the epitome of grace.

CONTENTS

PROLOGUE

It has been 5 years since we left Saudi Arabia. From the moment we left, I felt it was important to tell our story—to give others who are interested, but will never travel, a window into life in Saudi Arabia.

You may ask, "Why has it taken so long to put pen to paper?" I can certainly say that it is not because of a lack of effort. Whenever I would sit down and put my thoughts into perspective about Saudi Arabia, I generally found myself focusing on the parts that I disliked, as the laws there went against most things I stood for and believed in. The culture shock still has not entirely left me.

Had I written about my experiences when I first left, it would have been one-sided and negative to a large extent. While there are many things I still take issue with, I feel that it is important to be as objective as possible, allowing the reader to decide. There will be many times that I describe a situation as best as I can, which will include nationality, ethnicity, race, culture and context, as much as possible, to give the reader a vivid picture of the events that transpired. These are just my observations, which are intended to help make the strange familiar.

While the church and state in Saudi have been intertwined for many centuries, the unique culture of the country has added its own idiosyncrasies. Contrary to popular belief, Islam is not a single, racial group that is following a religion, but it is a religion that has many followers from most of the countries in the world. Numbers-wise, it is a close second to Christianity, in terms of followers.

That being said, religion is an idea, and no idea is beyond reproach. This memoir is, however, not a critique of Islam. Rather, it is a journey back through some of my experiences in Saudi Arabia and how they changed me. My hope is that my words will become a voice for so many who have been forced into silence.

CHAPTER 1
For Better or Worse

And without any more thought, the decision was made. We were going to Saudi Arabia. The decision was not an easy one, but our unique situation made it the only decision that would allow us to pay for past due credit cards, our home, medical bills, students loans and other miscellaneous debts that had started to accrue. I was unemployed and living in Michigan, which had one of the highest unemployment rates in the United States and one of the few states to boast a negative population rate after the stock market crash of 2008.

I studied and graduated from college with a double major in Marketing and English and was overjoyed to complete my studies, which were completed over a 5-year period. I saw my degrees as my ticket to a comfortable lifestyle, which included sports cars, flashy restaurants and tuxedoes.

My first job was at an online casino, and it introduced me to the torture of sitting in a cubicle and handling customer queries for 8 hours a day. Since the casino was a 24-hour enterprise, I worked all three shifts in a given month. While the job was soul-crushing and debilitating to my sense of karma, my salary made up for any feelings of remorse that would occasionally plague me. I convinced myself that I was not putting a gun to the clients' heads and that they were adults who were capable of making their own decisions.

I shrugged off my animosity towards the regimented corporate existence, promptly bought myself an Audi sports car and basked in my new-found, elevated status. However, the novelty wore off after a few weeks. I quickly realized that the car was just a car and did not make me feel any different, and I finally realized that I had bought into a consumer-driven world, whereby one's insatiable desires could be satisfied readily at the snap of a wallet clip.

Going to work and assisting clients/gambling addicts did not seem to pique my interest anymore. The wall I placed around myself in context to my ill feelings towards the industry began to surface in the blank thoughts I would usually have, while staring off into space. It was at about this time that I watched the movie, *Office Space*, which completely changed my outlook on life.

The movie was about a couple of employees who work at a large, corporate business and concluded that humans were not made for sitting in cubicles for half the waking day.

I went to work the next day determined to resign, but at the end of the day, I had talked myself out of what I had convinced myself was a rash decision. That was until I had my last call of the day...

A lady named Deborah called and said, "My house is about to be foreclosed on, and I need a free chip." Deborah was a regular gambler but had lost thousands of dollars in the last few months, and I could sense in her voice that she was desperate.

"Sorry, madam," I had to say. "It appears that you are not eligible for a free chip. I do apologize for the inconvenience."

"Please, Alex, my kids are starving, and I was recently laid off. I just need a free chip to make everything alright."

"I understand your predicament. I am sorry, but there is nothing that I can do." I felt awful.

It was at that moment that I felt my soul was completely blackened and had crossed a line that would forever define me if I continued to work in that industry. I stood up from my seat. My palms were clammy, and beads of sweat oozed out of my forehead. I began to walk towards the company director's office at a slow, steady pace, reminiscent of a condemned prisoner.

Placed on his office wall were framed posters of uplifting phrases and a picture of someone teeing off on a golf course, geared to motivate the team. All it needed was a can of instant cheese to spray on the walls and the mood would have been complete.

I stood in front of the desk that was cluttered with items that ranged from family pictures, an abacus, a Newton's cradle and a slinky. All the trappings of owning a business. Without wanting to delay or lose my nerve, I blurted out to him that I was resigning, effective that day.

It felt good. In fact, it was the best I had felt in a long time. I hoped that I would never put myself in that kind of predicament again, and life, though in a flux, was beautiful again.

Driving home, I turned my stereo up and blared Nirvana's cover of "Lake of Fire", thinking to myself how I had narrowly missed going to that towering inferno. I had no way of realizing that a similar feeling would rear its beautiful head at a future, pivotal junction in my life.

I spoke to my parents the following day, and they were absolutely disappointed with my decision to quit my job for two reasons that were repeated frequently: jobs were hard to come by, and I threw mine away without having a plan for the future.

For the first time, I realized that I might have to move back home! Independence, you were fleeting, and if only for that short period of time, you were my manna from heaven. I had to do something, quickly or risk taking a few steps too many in the wrong direction, regressing to a mid-twenties loser, living in his parents' basement.

Well, a few weeks later, I found myself living at home, and it wasn't so bad. The food was good, and the satellite T.V. kept me busy during the day for a few weeks. Being in my old stomping grounds, amongst friends and family, made me realize the importance of the quality of one's life, as opposed the sole acquisition of money. Granted, I did understand that one needs money to allow for a quality standard of living.

I played golf at least three times a week with my uncle who owned a successful business. Unlike my father, when I was a young adult, he dropped all adult like pretenses and talked and treated me like an equal. I grew to love my time spent with him and my first cousin, his son, on the golf course.

This made me conclude that even though I was not good at golf, I wanted to have a life that allowed for time during the day with friends and family. This positively reiterated my stance that I was not made to sit in a cubicle for eight to nine hours a day. There must be a job out there that could allow for a lifestyle that was without need of money yet still provide me with the ability to have leisure time. The problem was trying to locate this profession.

A business could be the answer, but I had no experience or interest in selling goods (which was odd, considering that my first major was marketing). My cooking skills were good, but again, I had no interest in starting a restaurant. I just felt that my passion would slowly become something I despised. Oh decisions, decisions... or lack of them to be brutally honest.

Teaching never interested me. My mother was an elementary teacher, and I witnessed her going through the monotony of the process, year in and year out. While she enjoyed the stability, I considered K-12 teaching to be another form of prison labor, stealing those precious daylight hours. A university professor position was my dream, but I found my undergraduate degree to be quite taxing on my mind, soul and self-respect in terms of my own perceived intelligence quotient. The thought of studying further at that moment of my life, literally left me sick to the stomach.

I felt like I needed to turn to a friend that had served me well throughout my life, both fueling and satiating my thirst for answers on a wide range of topics. I entered the library with the clear plan of not leaving there till I could find a job or a career that would check all the boxes for the quality of life I so yearned for. I was done with inactivity and told myself that I would not leave until I had some idea or direction in which to pursue.

For the first 30 minutes in the library, I reflected on how I had come to this impasse in my life. I was 25 years old, with a degree but still no closer to knowing what career and job I wanted. Having gone to a Catholic school, we were often told that everyone was endowed with skills or talents. It was our moral obligation to discover them, foster them and use them to guide us through life.

As a teenager, this was a daunting task and quite

a heavy burden for some. One almost felt like they were disappointing their Creator if they didn't find their talent. School, as in life, had people that knew exactly what they wanted to do after school, and then, there were those who didn't. I didn't know, when I was in school. I didn't know when I was in university either, and sitting in the library, I still didn't know. I made a mental note of one day addressing the lack of real career counseling at my high school, but that was a battle for another day. Today, I would stay at the library until I knew.

About an hour later, I was in the process of ordering my breakfast at a coffee shop when I bumped in to an acquaintance. A brief conversation ensued—both of us engaging in the societal tap-dance of inquiring after each's successes. The conversation was short on my part, but what he said turned out to be the most serendipitous moment of my entire life. Well, in hindsight, it was really the second most, but I will get to that later.

He briefly mentioned that he was teaching English as a second language in Korea, and he found the job to be very rewarding. He referred to his career choice as a working vacation. Working vacation? My eyes lit up. That phrase summed up everything I hoped and desired from a job. But it was teaching. I inquired about the long, dull repetition of a day that was synonymous with teaching, and I was pleasantly surprised to find out that he only taught 4 hours a day.

With renewed vigor, I returned to the library and found as much research as possible pertaining to finding a job overseas, teaching, expat living, etc. Within a week, I had applied for and accepted a teaching position in Korea and was in the country the following week. I looked forward to a life of travel, intrigue and new possibilities that I could never have conceived of while sitting in my parents' basement.

South Korea was all that I had imagined and more. I met my wife, Liz (the most serendipitous moment of my life to date and deserves its own story), discovered a passion for teaching and matured to realize that while I pursued a life of quality, I had arrogantly put undue stress on my family by my rash decision to leave my job without first working through an alternate plan for my future. I would never do that again.

Career counselors can be a dangerous bunch. Liz found this out the hard way. In high school, she was fed the truism that she should pursue a career that allowed her to do something that she loved. She loved to paint and was encouraged to dive head first into a $60,000 art degree that would ensure that she would be paying it back for the rest of her life—all because the counselor neglected to mention that she would be gainfully unemployed for the rest of her life.

Her particular counselor was a hopeless career romantic who felt that with enough prayer and perseverance, one could achieve anything. The old adage that persistence is the key was proudly stenciled onto her door. We were so saturated with this message at school that it became akin to an axiom math problem: Passion plus perseverance equals rewards—the American way.

Reality struck when she left college and bounced around minimum wage jobs at Starbucks and catering to being a docent (unpaid) at a gallery, which was the first job she could be proud to say was a direct result of having an art degree. The second job she got with her art degree proved to be the last.

She got a customer care position at a printing business. The owner, a narcissistic, "holier than thou", self-made millionaire often came to her workstation during the first week of her employment to discuss how he did not have a degree, yet he had amassed a fortune. "The Lord has found favor with me and has blessed me..." were the final words he chanted before going to a lunch off premises for the rest of the day, on a daily basis.

After a week of working there, the staff was told that the business was going through a rough patch and wages would need to be cut. This coincided with a delivery of a Lamborghini to the storefront. For the following week, he drove the vehicle to work, calling any employee close by to take a look at how the Lord had blessed him.

The mood got so somber that one person contemplated burning down the store. While it was said in jest, another employee merely pointed out that he would make more money from his fire insurance. Truly blessed was he.

The next day, Liz was let go, due to the low productivity of the business, and another employee had to do the work of 2 people. This was the breaking point in her trying to find a career where her true passion laid, and she decided to teach. If you can't do (granted she wasn't ever given the chance to do), teach, and it certainly paid better than all of her previous jobs. She tried her hand at substituting, seeing if teaching was a good fit, and she found it palatable.

One day, in the staffroom, she overheard a few teachers talking about a friend who was teaching in South Korea and having a great time. Liz enjoyed traveling and did not mind teaching, so this interested her.

As soon as she went home, she researched teaching in Korea, applied for a job and was off on her adventure 3 months later. We met, got married and, like a sinister déjà vu, we both found ourselves in the same predicament prior to teaching in Korea. Birds of a feather...

After a year of teaching in Korea, we made the decision to return to the states and find gainful employment, thus beginning our life as our parents had done before. There was just one problem: There were little to no jobs, and the 2008 recession showed little signs of losing its grip.

After meandering from one call center job to

another debt collection job, I realized that my life went full circle, and I was in a worse predicament than my previous attempt at finding a career, prior to going to Korea. I needed to find a solution as the bills started mounting.

"Depression"—not an easy word to say out aloud. The type I had could not be cured or alleviated with therapy or pharmaceutical drugs. Having grown up in a religious family, the doctrine of the male being the head of the household and the breadwinner was branded on my soul. Being married and not having the ability to support my wife made me feel like I had let down my family and my community.

When we were at church, I would feel the eyes of people looking down at me, and when asked (and I was asked weekly) if I had found a job, I would just talk about continuing my studies. I wasn't really continuing my studies, for I did not want to dig myself into another financial hole. It seemed, to most people, the solution was to throw more money at the problem, pray and all would be okay.

I needed a job, and I needed to make money. I tried my hand at several temp positions, and I can say with authority that if you need a person to mechanically separate chicken, I am your guy.

I was at an age when I began to feel like the world was passing me by. Friends of mine who found jobs after college were well into managerial positions with 401k's, dental, etc. I was at the starting line, and my next job needed to be something that not only furthered my experience in my chosen field but also paid well enough. It was getting to be too tough to live without a living wage.

My final job in the States was supposed to be the job that ended all jobs. I was courted by a nonprofit organization to teach English to immigrants. The focus was to give them a fighting chance at being successful in the workplace. This would have a snowball effect of uplifting their lives and helping their dreams become a reality. It was a noble cause. I knew I could do this job for decades and not become bored with empowering families. However, there was one hitch: At the final stage of my interview, it was indicated that they would like to move forward with me, so we discussed money. I was offered less than my factory chicken-separating job.

The interviewer spoke passionately. "We are a nonprofit and cannot compete with corporate companies. What we do offer you is a chance to change the lives of many. It is not often that we get resumes with your international teaching experience, and you will be an asset. Thank you for applying, and thank you making your skills available to those in need."

I felt like I had been punched in the gut. I was asked to be a beacon of hope to many, while living on something close to minimum wage. I did not think I had the ability to do this. My debt far outweighed my salary. I went home further depressed, and after a quick Google search, I found out that the interviewer was the director of the institute. She was earning over $130,000 a year. I guess the institute, though a nonprofit, could complete and surpass corporate wage expectations to have her at the helm. With all being said, I thought that the job could be the foundation of a new career, and the growth could be limitless.

The next day, I got a call from the assistant director to tell me that the position was offered to someone else. I inquired as to how I could have interviewed better. The assistant director broke all pretenses and commenced to tell me that she wanted to employ me, but the director wanted to give the job to a friend who did not have a degree, which meant that the department would save money.

After hearing about what had happened, Liz said, "Well, it sounds like a job created specifically for a privileged housewife who is tired of spending her husband's money. Not much pay, but it comes with a title and the adoration of the masses."

I knew she was trying to save my feelings at the expense of her own feminine lib. "House person, hmmm...? I would have gladly accepted the honor of that job," I replied. Self-deprecating to uplift another, that was love. I made a note to repay the good turn at the first opportunity.

Liz continued, "And you know that this city is

an old boys' club with jobs only for family friends. When I interned at the local community college for a month, working in the academic outreach department for immigrants, just about everyone working in the department did not apply for the position they were working in. The lead instructor was friends with the program assistant prior to getting her job. Instructors/friends were hired for the semester, and then official job postings went out a few months later. Many professional jobs were posted just to conform to labor laws."

She looked up to see if I was still listening, and I nodded for her to continue. "It was obviously illegal by the way it was done, but the department did not have a union or anyone to which they could raise their concerns. I found this interesting that the program assistant would do the academic dean's job, since he was either hiding out in an office 30 miles away or on the golf course. The program assistant figured herself as a champion of the masses, posting her activism on Facebook at every opportunity. You know the type. The irony was lost on her."

Liz sighed. "I think the worse part was that this was a department run on a grant, yet 90% of the students were from the program assistant's country of heritage. I know for a fact that there are people from many other countries that live in the area who would have benefitted from the program, but with no one holding anyone accountable, nepotism, racism and prejudice practices were the norm."

She paused a moment, lost in thought, and then said contemplatively, "I do recall that there was one instructor, the only one in all of the departments, that was hired through a legitimate hiring process. However, he started asking awkward questions about the program. Suffice it to say, he did not last long, even though he had the best student pass rates. According to his Facebook page, he is now between jobs."

This was the nail in the coffin, and at that moment, it was obvious to both of us that another stint, teaching overseas, was our only option. I decided that I wanted to teach overseas again, but this time as a mercenary, selling myself to the highest bidder.

Saudi Arabia won, and in one week, I had secured an English teaching job and a free flight to the destination for myself and for my Liz.

Saudi Arabia had an interesting visa system. While you could get a visa to go on a pilgrimage (*Hajj*) into Mecca, technically, there were no tourist visas. One could argue that besides the *Hajj*, there was not much to see, since Saudi was not geared towards facilitating tourism around the country. The process to get a work visa, called an *iqama*, was a long and laborious process. One had to do a battery of medical tests, application forms (sometimes in triplicate), bank statements for 3 months, a job offer contract, a flight ticket, a hotel booking for when you arrive, travel medical insurance and the list goes on and on, depending on which country you are from.

With most things in Saudi, there was a visa loophole, to get workers in the country without going through the whole *iqama* process. Worker turnover was high, so there was a serious need to replace workers as soon as possible. The visiting professional visa was created for highly skilled leaders in their fields who wished to hold seminars, train workers, etc. It was not meant to be used as a work visa, per se, but that is what it became.

Instead of an average 6-month turnover for the *iqama*, the visiting professional visa took between one to two weeks to get. It was valid for 3 months, but while in the country, it could be renewed indefinitely. The teaching company we would be employed with favored the latter visa.

As luck would have it, the period leading up to our departure was fraught with visa issues and a foreboding sense of unease. Our updated visas in our passports arrived within two weeks of sending it off to the Saudi Arabian Embassy in Washington D.C., but my name was incorrectly spelled. This meant that I had to send off my visa back to the embassy to get it redone. This coincided with the build-up towards the holy month of Ramadan, and the embassy was inundated with visa requests.

Suffice to say, it took the better part of two

months to receive my updated visa. All the while, we began to question our decision. Our financial predicament remained the same, which was the main driving force to find a paying job in what was considered to be the most restrictive country in the world.

The visa delay had an unexpected positive drawback in that it gave us the opportunity to celebrate Thanksgiving and say our final good-byes to both family and friends during this period when most were off from work.

The day after Thanksgiving, Liz wandered off to the mailbox and brought home a surprise. Our visas had arrived! I was shocked halfway to death with surprise, as we had no more excuses to prolong our trip.

Fun and excitement soon enveloped us as we were nearing another adventure. I realized, for better or worse, my dream of becoming a university professor was about to be fulfilled. Little did we know that our thoughts, mindset and future actions would be irreparably altered from our experiences in Saudi Arabia. We would become drawn into a false sense of security, brought about by a thin façade of normality. We would witness the strong tug between traditional and modernistic thinking, colliding on a daily basis. We would come to know and understand the people that were both victims and promoters of a jingoist education system and autocratic religious government that instilled hate, racism and prejudice on young and impressionable people. We also would discover the underbelly of human rights violations that continue to go unchecked today.

CHAPTER 2
For Poorer or Richer

"I'm going to tell you what everyone is thinking, but what everyone is too afraid to say: You guys are crazy. Nuts! How can you go to Saudi Arabia? Do you know that they have that Sharia Law? Man, I wouldn't go there even if you paid me!" Jon exclaimed as soon as he entered our home.

"Well, that's why we are going: to get paid," I replied.

Liz had invited over her oldest friend, Karen, and her outspoken husband, Jon, followed in tow. Truth be told, Jon wasn't far off the mark. I sensed by the looks I was getting from family over the last few weeks that there was much left unsaid. Our family understood our predicament and our decision. While they did not agree with it, they understood. Jon did not have that luxury. Jon spoke his mind regardless of the situation. In the black and white manner that he perceived the world, the cliché "out of the mouths of babes" came to mind.

I continued, "Yes, we understand, more or less,

what we are getting ourselves into. I guess we will understand the full magnitude of our decision when we get there. Could I interest you in a beer, Jon?"

"You do know that there is no alcohol in Saudi, and if you are caught drinking, you can get whipped."

"I read that somewhere. I may have a solution for that, but we will see how it goes and play it by ear," I replied.

"Speaking about body parts, I heard that if you are caught or even suspected of stealing, they will chop your arm off." Jon accepted the beer offering, without much of a pause between sentences. "The other day I read a story about a hotel guest who claimed that his cellphone was missing from his room. He complained to the manager and continued with his day. The next day while packing, he found his cellphone under the bed. When he checked out, he mentioned this to the manager who just said, 'It's okay. The problem was sorted.' The guest later found out that the maid who cleaned the room was taken to the police, and with the swift justice of Saudi, she was armless less than 24 hours later. True story!"

I nodded. "Hmm, yes, we've heard similar stories as well. Don't you think it's a bit of a hyperbole? Let's get you set up with another beer, Jon."

After Karen and Jon left, I felt for the first time a sense of anxiety about our flight to Saudi the next day. Sitting down, I suppressed those feelings with a can of Milwaukee's Best Beer. Looking at the can brought the move into perspective again. We were close to being destitute, and cheap beer was all I could afford. I wasn't entirely sure that buying it was a good way to spend what little money we had, but it did dull my senses for the evening—well worth it in the end.

Liz continued to pack in a slow, determined fashion, hoping not to forget anything. "Do you think we can take the Bible? Do you think we should risk it? I read that we can take one holy book. My biggest fear is that they will go through our luggage and prosecute us for anything they may consider contraband."

"According to the Saudi government website, it's okay. Take it. Who knows when we may need inspiration?" I said.

After a restless night of sleep, filled with face-less shadows, we woke up bright and early for our flight.

"Here are your tickets, and don't forget that alcohol is free on international flights. Also, the food choices are excellent," the attendant at the airport said, with a little wink. "Enjoy your trip, and please be sure to choose us again."

After some heartfelt goodbyes with our family, Liz and I made our way through the security gates and onto the plane.

"So, where is your final destination?" asked the airhost.

"Saudi Arabia," replied Liz.

"Oh my! You guys do know that there is no alcohol allowed there, right? I would never survive…"

Liz and I would categorize ourselves as social drinkers, with an odd overindulgence here and there, but the focus on the lack of alcohol in Saudi Arabia seemed to be an ever-present discussion point, even amongst acquaintances that did not indulge. I was beginning to think that the lack of alcohol was a euphemism for what others had perceived as a lack of freedom.

In America, the word "freedom" often got thrown around as one of the defining differences that separated us from the world. The thought of not having the freedom of choice to consume whatever one desired seemed to bother those around us more than it did us.

I began to wonder. Our extensive travel around the world had shown us that freedom was not the exception, uncommon and unique but more so the rule. I felt that just like the USA had introduced prohibition in the 1920s, Saudi Arabia had its reasons, and who was I to judge? I'm not sure if my nonchalant attitude was a wall I had created in my mind to cope with our move, or if I was truly open to understanding if the country was as repressive as it was reported in the media. This was a question that I hoped to answer for myself.

Our flight left Chicago en route to Riyadh, via Abu Dhabi, at 8pm. We flew with Etihad Airlines and were totally amazed at the food selection, the range of beverages, the quality of movies and the vast music selection. We were used to feeling like inconvenient cattle on domestic flights, so even though we were sitting in coach, we felt like business class kings. Why couldn't all air travel be like this?

Liz mentioned that this could be our proverbial "last meal/drink" before Saudi, so we decided to test the efficacy of the airhost in responding to drink orders. I almost felt like we were in the calm before the storm, but a storm that we had no real idea of how to prepare for.

After 3 drinks, the final of which being consumed at around 11pm, the airhost mentioned that they had an altercation with a customer on the previous flight, and they would be capping the allocated drinks to 3 for the evening. I supposed, then, that was a good time, if any, to go to sleep. However, with adrenaline pumping through my body, I found it difficult to sleep. When sleep did come, it was filled with nonsensical dream scenes and then finally a black void.

I was woken by a monotonous voice over the intercom, informing the passengers that we were 2 hours from our destination. We disembarked from the airplane and found the closest Wi-Fi hotspot. We had four hours to wait for our connecting flight to Riyadh, so we decided to relax and get lost in cyberspace.

We were sitting in a common area, and many

people came and left over the course of an hour. All was quiet and peaceful, until we heard loud yelling behind us. A man dressed in traditional Arab clothing was screaming at the top of his voice at another man who had his hands up, obviously not understanding what was transpiring. Another man, sitting close to us, raised his hand and waved the confused soul to come towards where we were.

"Are you okay? Come, take a seat here..."

"What just happened?"

"You are not a member of his family, and by the looks of it, you sat next to his wife."

"This place is full. I was under the impression that it was common space."

"There is common space, and then there is Arabian space. You will do well to know the difference. In Arabian culture, an unrelated male cannot sit at the same table when there are females present. While they don't demarcate it in this airport, it is a cultural rule. Where is your final destination?"

"Saudi Arabia."

When Liz and I heard this, we both turned our heads and listened intently, wondering if we were going to be bestowed with some pearls of wisdom.

"Saudi, same here. I have been working there for the last couple of years. As a single male, you need to be mindful that eating places in restaurants and malls are segregated in terms of family and single men. If you sit in the family section, even un-knowingly, they can incarcerate you. I'm told that the jails in Saudi are a hell of a place, and the *kapsa* is dry."

"What is *kapsa*?"

"My poor attempt at humor. *Kapsa* is the national dish of Saudi. It is comprised of roasted chicken on a bed of rice. Just about every restaurant has it on their menu."

"Thank you very much for all the information. You've been very helpful and kind."

Liz and I looked at each other with raised eyebrows. Having eavesdropped on that conversation would later prove to be quite helpful to us. It also made us contemplate how many other cultural rules we were going to need to learn, and quickly.

About an hour later, we boarded our connecting flight to Saudi. Even though the flight was just under two hours long, it was, without a doubt, the most interesting flight we had ever been on—interesting for all the wrong reasons.

When the gate opened for boarding the plane, we joined the hastily made line. Then, as if the line did not exist, people started pushing ahead and cutting in. The hustling and tussling only got worse, and I was sure that our flight would be cancelled if this continued. It was sheer chaos.

Liz looked on in horror. "We have our seats assigned to us, and that cannot change. Let's get the hell out of the line!"

We took a seat and watched the drama unfold. The concept of a line seemed foreign to the group of people, pushing each other to get on a plane with predetermined seating. Did it really matter if you were first or last? Both Liz and I went to K-12 religiously affiliated schools that beat in the idea of discipline and order. Forming a line when leaving and coming back to class after break and for all formal events was one of the very first rules we had learned. We had always been told that without discipline and order, chaos would prevail. While I did scoff at it as fear mongering at the time, I could now see firsthand why the simple act of learning to form a line was one of most important forms of societal decorum. However, this seemed to be the norm to the airhosts at the gate, and eventually, the crowd started to thin out.

When we finally walked onto the plane, a pungent aroma hit us. The smell was reminiscent of how I smelled after seven days of backcountry backpacking in Isle Royale National Park, Michigan.

As we proceeded into the cabin, looking for our seats, the aroma seemed to multiply with every step. I turned back to confirm our seat numbers with Liz, and her face was flushed.

"Are you okay?" I asked her.

"I think I'm going to throw up," she replied.

"Looks like we are almost to our seats. Once we sit down, you can see how you feel," I said.

We sat down, and the aroma seemed to

strengthen. It smelled like an animal crawled up someone's armpit, died and also pooped itself in its last throws of life.

Liz was barely hanging on. I looked up at Liz's headrest. The male passenger, dressed in dusty, traditional, Middle Eastern slacks, sitting behind us, had his hands placed firmly on her headrest. I asked if he wouldn't mind moving his hands.

He looked at Liz and asked, "Wife? Wife?"

I answered, "Yes."

He quickly moved his hands off her headrest, lifted them in a sign of surrender and apologized profusely, saying, "Oh, sawrry, sawrrrry..."

I mentioned that it was okay, but he continued to apologize. At that point, the poop smell disappeared, and my mind was allowed to briefly process the situation. I had once read that in the Middle East some people frequent an Eastern toilet and use a hand-held shower to wash the excrement, whilst using their hand as toilet paper. While I didn't entirely believe it when I read it, I felt that I now had my firsthand (pun not intended) experience of this phenomenon. I certainly was not one to judge anybody's culture, but I did not want to have poop on my hands either.

I often took acid reducers for a gastric reflux problem, and with the reduction in stomach acid, I was more prone to stomach and bowel ailments. Would it be possible to get through this adventure without shaking a single hand? Would this impact me in a negative manner? Only time would tell.

The airhost walked up and down the aisles, liberally spraying air freshener—another first. Liz hated air freshener of any sort and had banned it from our home, but at this moment, the color began to return to her pale face. It was as if the air freshener was a breath of fresh air. Allergies be damned, we could breathe again. We didn't throw up that day, but getting upset stomachs was something that we would get quite accustomed to over the course of the year.

This was the first time that we were on a plane with the majority of people not wearing western clothing. Our journey had officially begun, and we were in the realm of the unknown.

Liz pulled out her culture guide of Saudi Arabia and began digesting the information with fervor.

"I wish I started this earlier," she said. "Looks like I have to walk behind you when we walk in the public."

"Well, you are my property and/or under my protection. I can protect you much better if you were behind me," I replied.

"Save your jokes," she said. "I'm still recovering from your brilliant suggestion to watch the movie *Not without My Daughter* last week. I think what freaked me out the most was that she was from Michigan. That made it all too real…"

"Oh, Liz, it will be okay," I said, attempting to sound believable. "We will just put our heads down, follow the rules and get ourselves out of debt as quickly as possible."

"Maybe I should just go to the bathroom and put on my *abaya*. I'm not sure if I will have the opportunity later."

"Might as well," I replied.

When Liz came back from the bathroom, she seamlessly sat down and asked, "Do I look like a penguin? Pale, anemic-looking face and a black *abaya*?"

"A few days in the desert should change that anemic look," I mentioned.

"Yes, and give me more wrinkles?" remarked Liz.

For the rest of the flight, Liz read, while I got lost in nostalgia. The last time I left the country to take up a teaching job overseas was 3 years before. That decision proved to be one of the best, if not the best, decision I had made in my adult life. I had grown as an individual and befriended wonderful people from all over the globe. The experience had profound and lifelong ramifications. I began wondering if I was about to embark on a similar adventure.

When the plane landed, we decided to hang back and wait for most of the people to disembark. This did not happen straight away, since the plane needed to complete its taxiing procedure. An individual decided to remove his seat belt and sprint towards the entrance of the plane. He crouched down and lowered his head, hoping not to be seen.

Over the speaker system, an airhostess gave a general announcement, informing the passengers that they must have their seatbelts on. The individual looked around then put his head down again. A minute later, the loud booming voice of the captain made it clear that the door would not open unless everyone was in his or her seats. The individual kept his head down. I am not sure if he understood the captain, but passengers started getting irate, screaming directions at him. The individual ignored everyone and remained crouched.

Another minute went by, and the captain had an airhost who spoke Arabic go to him and inform him that no one would get off the plane unless he went back to his seat. At least that was what the guy next to me told me. The individual reluctantly stood up and headed back to his seat sporadically getting heckled along the way.

Eventually, we exited the plane and were hit by an icy coldness.

"We are in a desert, right?" Liz inquired, visibly confused.

"I guess it's true what they say about the desert: When it's hot, it's very hot, and when it's cold, it's frigid."

We walked into the terminal and toward the baggage claim area. Liz began to get nervous.

"Do you think we packed anything that can be construed as contraband?"

It was 3:30 in the morning, and I was exhausted.

I think if it was earlier in the evening, I would have had an elevated level of adrenalin, but as it stood, I was too tired to think. Ahead of me was a guy who looked Saudi but had an American passport, so I struck up a conversation while waiting to pass through customs.

"What's your name?" he asked after I commented that I was from the USA as well.

"Alex. Yourself?" I replied.

"Yousef. Ah, you probably here for business or teaching."

"Teaching, quite astute."

"Not really. Saudi does not have vacation visas, unless you are Muslim and are here on pilgrimage. You do not have a Muslim name, so you must be here to earn a living."

"You gauged all of that from asking me my name?" I asked.

"Yes. When you first speak to people that are Muslim here, most will ask you your name just so that they know whether you are Muslim or not. Common practice. Most people who hear you are not Muslim will see it as a sign as not to speak about religious matters with you. I see it as a way of respecting another person. You won't find door-to-door Muslims like the Jehovah's Witnesses back home. Anyway, have a wonderful stay and visit some of the *souks* dotted around the city. In case you were wondering, a *souk* is a large, open-air market with many interesting wares."

"Thank you, Yousef. I will look into that," I said,

gratefully.

After clearing the first round of customs, Liz's fears were quickly swept aside. When were we arrived at the exit section of the airport, the person manning the x-ray machine was asleep. We put some bags on the escalator to follow the rules, and when no one attended to them, politely picked up our bags and walked out the airport.

We had built-up this moment for months, working through it in our heads, and it ended up being a nonevent. I hoped that this trend would continue for the rest of the year.

At the entrance of the airport, a man in Saudi traditional clothes, held a sign with our names on it. This was another huge sigh of relief, since all we wanted to do was get to a bed and sleep for a day.

Liz was especially nervous. When she arrived in South Korea to teach English, nobody came to pick her up, and she had to make her own arrangements.

The driver greeted us with a warm smile and offered to help us with our bags. Our bags just managed to fit in his Toyota Yaris, and off we went.

As we left the airport, we noticed that there were huge puddles of water on the sides of the road, and the city looked well soaked.

"We are in desert, right?" Liz inquired, looking bewildered.

"Makes you wonder..." I replied.

"Maybe we will see some desert flowers bloom in the next couple of weeks."

It was at the moment that Liz and I noticed that the driver had his foot down on the accelerator and was approaching 100 miles per hour. Traveling at this breakneck speed on a wet road was not a good idea. The strange thing was that other cars were passing us. We hit a large puddle of water in the middle of the three-lane highway, and our car hydroplaned to the left lane. Thank goodness there was nobody else in that lane.

Liz turned and said frantically, "This guy has a death wish. Tell him to slow down! Please, tell him to slow down!"

I'm not sure if he heard Liz or came to his senses, but he slowed down to 70 mph and held two hands firmly on the wheel.

This form of high-speed driving was our first introduction to driving in Saudi. We were soon to find out that when one entered a car in Saudi, they were taking their lives into their own hands. Streetlights and signs would rarely be adhered to and were seen as advisory.

Drifting (taking a turn at a high speed so the back wheels of the car slide around the bend) was often done on the city roads, some congested. It would not be uncommon for pedestrians to be run over.

I wondered if the fear of getting killed was the reason for a general lack of pedestrians on the road. I would later find out that there was more to this, as well. Saudi was an onion with many layers. Three-lane highways quickly became five as people drove in the emergency shoulder lanes to get ahead of the traffic.

The driver escorted us to what he described as a hotel, but it had more of an apartment feel to it, with two baths and two bedrooms. The apartment had an old, dusty feel, even though it was less than five years old. This observation became a commonplace phenomenon as most buildings in the suburbs had an old feel, even though they were new, due to frequent dust storms and poor workmanship. It also seemed that a majority of buildings did not seem to adhere to any proper building codes.

We were looking forward to a long nap and just wanted to get to the apartment. As we walked past the front desk, the attendant began to talk in a fast pace, pointing at us. The driver turned to us and said that the attendant needed to get a copy of our marriage certificate, as unmarried couples were not allowed to cohabitate in an apartment.

Liz, ever prepared, pulled out our marriage certificate, and the attendant proceeded to make a copy. I looked at the certificate again, this time upside down, and it became obvious that he could not read English. A mischievous part of me thought that anyone could fake a marriage certificate and come to Saudi as a "couple".

There were definitely many more benefits to coming to Saudi as a couple, as opposed to being single. The housing and car allowance was higher; couples did not have to share a room with a stranger; single men were not allowed in malls; many restaurants only had a "family" section, meaning no single men, and the list went on.

We were finally escorted to our room, and the driver indicated that he would come the following day to take us to the main education office. We both thought that was a kind gesture, especially since it was past 4am. We went directly to our bed, and without talking, we fell into a dreamless sleep.

((Bang! Bang!)) "Hello, how you?!" ((Bang! Bang!))

I lifted my head off the pillow in a shocked state. How long did we sleep for? What time was it? Did we sleep for an entire day?

((Bang! Bang! Bang!))

Liz jumped off the bed, looking discombobulated, turning her head from one side to the next. "Is someone trying to break in?" she shrieked.

"It's 8am! Did we sleep for the entire day and night?"

"Hello, must go office now, hello."

"We only slept for 3 hours!"

"I thought they were coming tomorrow..." said Liz.

"Lost in translation I guess," I replied.

I slowly shuffled to the door and opened it.

"Bring bags. Everything and everything. We go office."

"So, we must pack our suitcases and take everything?"

"Everything, everything. I wait in van. You come."

"Okay," I said. "We'll meet you at the van in five minutes."

"Okayee... okayee..."

"Liz, we have to pack everything and go."

"What?! No," said Liz. "I'm a walking, talking zombie. I want to go back to bed. Tell him to come back tomorrow."

"Wish I could. He has gone back to the van and is waiting for us."

"Oh my word! Can this just end!?"

"Okay, let's just get this over with."

We hurriedly packed our bags and departed the "hotel".

The minibus was full except for the backseat. We loaded our bags in the rear and shuffled our way to our seat. We were both extremely jet-lagged and just wanted to rest our eyes, when a lady in the front seat started talking to no one in particular.

"Arabic is the most beautiful language. I understand why it is God's chosen language. He created perfection. In Heaven, we will all be speaking Arabic. You, me, even Julia Roberts," she remarked.

"Where are you from?" asked a guy in the middle row.

"Turkey, yourself?"

"Philly, born and bred," he replied ecstatically.

"Where is that?" she looked puzzled.

"The U.S. of A..." he said proudly, with per-plexed look on his face. It was almost as if he was inferring that everyone should know about Phila-delphia.

"Ah, you are American. You guys tend to think that people know every city, as if they were na-tive. I'm from Ankara. Have you heard of that city?

"No, but I would like to hear more about it," he replied, while licking his lips.

She smiled at him and began regaling her thoughts on her city, only stopping to take a breath of air from time to time.

As if he was mesmerized, he looked longingly at her while she spoke.

I found it interesting that he was wearing the traditional Saudi garb. This was the first time that I saw a westerner in Saudi garb. The next few days, I would learn that many foreigners wear the trad-itional garments called *thobes*. *Thobes* were white and resembled dresses. Since this was the desert, it made sense to wear them, because they were cool and airy. I made a mental note to look into purchasing one.

While the Turkish lady continued to give her thoughts on other matters, I began to nod off to sleep, but was stirred when the minibus came to an abrupt stop.

"Looks like we have arrived. Finally! I hope this

doesn't turn into a waiting session," said Liz.

I asked the driver where we should go exactly, since the building was a large double-story.

"In, in, top, back," he replied. "Easy, easy."

I realized he was trying his best, so I nodded my head as if I understood, and Liz and I headed into the building. The building was white and shaped like a large box with windows—a typical design for the area.

At the entrance of the building, a person stood behind a desk. Thinking that he was a customer service rep, I told him that we were new teachers and wanted to know where to go and who to see. The person behind the desk pointed towards a lift and said, "Up, up, back."

Having "spoken" to two people, we gathered that we needed to go upstairs and find our way to the back of the building. Getting out of the lift, we made our way to the back of the building, but this proved to be a little difficult as the area was a maze with many passageways. We walked around, trying to find anyone to help us, but the building seemed like it was evacuated. Liz headed towards a water fountain, and I decided to look for someone, anyone, in the front section of the second floor.

I went back downstairs, and the person behind the desk was gone. The hair on the back of my neck stood up, and I felt a weird sensation overwhelm my body. I was confused and began to feel a growing sense of fear. I enjoyed reading macabre and dystopian novels, but none of that seemed to prepare me for this moment. For a building this size, at 1pm in the afternoon, there had to be someone around. The lack of sleep and jetlag was not making matters any better, and I decided to go back upstairs and share my findings with Liz.

When I arrived at the water fountain, Liz was nowhere to be found. I heard a toilet flush and a few seconds later, Liz came out of an unmarked bathroom.

"I had to go. I think this was a male's bathroom, though. Do you think I can go to jail for that if I was caught?" Liz asked jokingly.

"I'm not sure, but I don't think you should do that again," I responded.

"Whatever. Where are these people? It feels like there is going to be a zombie apocalypse at any minute..."

Just as Liz mentioned that, someone came up the flight of stairs.

"Hi!" I said. "Where is everyone?"

"Gone to mosque. It was the call to prayer. Get used to that. Everything shuts down about 5 times a day, though in the morning prayer doesn't usually effect business, since it's early. Anyway, my name is Mustafa. I work here. Let me guess... new teachers?"

"Yes," I replied.

"Well, you are probably looking for Osmah."

My eyes went wide. Not sure if he was joking, I laughed nervously.

"Isn't he in Afghanistan?" Liz asked.

Mustafa laughed and said that the coordinator of new teacher placement was named Osmah, and his office was in the back part of the building on the left corner. Now it all made sense. The broken directions we received had indicated that we should find who we were looking for in that general direction.

We knocked on the door and heard a strong, booming voice, indicating we should enter. Behind the desk was tall, large man. He stood up, shook our hands and asked us to sit. After asking us about our flight, we got down to business and were told that I would be at the men's university, King Saud, and Liz would be at the ladies' university, Princess Nora.

Liz asked if there was any co-ed university, where we could work together, and he mentioned that it would be a possibility in a few decades. I burst out laughing, and Liz gave me the biggest bug eyes I had ever received.

Getting straight to the point, as if he had done it a thousand times before (with the high teacher turnover rate, this could have been close to the truth), Osmah walked us through how and when we would be paid, wiring our money overseas and finally our living arrangements.

We were told that our new apartment was not ready, and the driver would drop us off at the same place we came from. He then gave us his business card and instructed, "Two days till you move into your new apartment. You will start school once you are set up there. For now, just don't get into any trouble." Osmah smiled, as he walked us to the door of his office.

We walked back to the minivan, and upon arriving "home", we unloaded our bags and went straight to bed for the longest sleep in history.

"Wake up, Rip!" Liz ordered while shaking me violently.

"Uhh, who's Rip?"

"You are! You have slept over 14 hours."

"Why Rip?" I asked as I urged myself to wake up with a prolonged stretch.

"Van Winkel. Don't you know the story...?"

"Yeah, it comes to me. It sounds like a Dutch name. Maybe he was just high and imagined he slept for decades."

"I highly doubt anyone from around here will find that funny. Anyway, I'm hungry. Get out there and find me some food."

"What!?!" I replied with mock horror and confusion.

The time had finally come to brave our new world and go forth into the unknown. I changed into what I would consider conservative attire: jeans, sweater and sneakers. I walked out onto the street, while Liz stayed behind to organize our belongings a bit.

The apartment building was at the end of a small CBD (central business district), and there were rows of stores and eateries all the way up the road. The building looked weather-beaten from the constant sand blasting, and newly painted buildings (usually white) developed a light brown color after a few weeks.

I proceeded to walk up the street and noticed that it was almost empty. I checked my watch, and it was almost midday. Either this was a night-life culture, or I was smack in the middle of a call to prayer. Both answers proved to be true, but for now, I needed to find out what time the store would open again. I went back to the apart-ment lobby and asked the attendant what time the stores would open. He seemed to understand some of what I was saying and mentioned, 10 minutes, holding his hands up.

Since the streets were sparsely populated at the time, I thought that it was a good idea to walk the main strip and look for stores of interest. Liz had asked me to be on the lookout for a clothing store as her university dress code enforced a conserva-tive, no leg, elbow or cleavage view.

The first takeout I happened upon was a fa-lafel eatery. They offered many combos, which in-cluded falafels, fries, boiled eggs, pickled cabbage, parsley salad and a variety of other delightful additions. The platter that included something of everything was only $4. I could get used to these prices. A meal with a few falafels was usual double the price in the States. I made a mental note of the store and continued to walk the strip.

I happened on a few more interesting eateries and a small clothing store. It seemed like this area provided all we needed within a short distance. Did we really need to move?

As I strolled along the strip, I noticed more and more people on the street. It was as if the world was waking from its slumber. One by one, the stores started opening, and by the time I walked to the end of the street and did a u-turn back towards the apartment, the strip was buzzing with activity.

I was the first customer at the store and pointed at the combo I desired and said that one please. To my amazement, the cashier replied in English, first acknowledging my choice and then asking where I was from. I mentioned the USA and asked him likewise.

"Syria. Most us working in the store is Syrian. War is *mushkala*, but over soon," he replied.

"I hope so to. You must miss your family."

"Yes," he replied.

"Your English is good. Where did you learn it?"

"In school. Everyone study English. Here is food. *Shukran*, my friend."

"Thank you," I replied, taking custody of a huge platter. It looked like we had breakfast, lunch and dinner.

I knocked on the apartment door, and for the first time, I noticed that it was made of steel. Was it to keep people in or out? I pondered that for a second until I heard a confused voice behind the door asking who was there.

"Have you forgotten that you sent me forth into the world to convert the masses?" I joked.

"You really need to get a filter for your brain," Liz teased back as she opened the door. "Come in. Anyway, where is the food? I'm starving."

Over the delicious meal, I relayed all that I saw. The food seemed to give Liz an injection of Dutch courage, and after we were done, we both ventured into the street. As we walked out of the apartment, a lady walking down the stairs said hello and asked if we were new teachers. We simultaneously said yes, and the lady's eyes lit up.

"I didn't realize that there were any more teachers in the building. They have been moving us out for the last few weeks to a new building," she explained. The other teachers have complained that the new building is in the middle of nowhere with few amenities. I have been holding out, but I was told that a driver will pick me up tomorrow. We must be going there together," she mentioned in a hurried voice.

"Oh, mind my manners! I'm Gina, from England."

After our introductions, and a brief chat, Liz and I hit the streets.

"We are in a city, but the dust is everywhere," Liz remarked.

"Probably got something to do with being in a desert," I replied.

"I have had just enough out of you, mister boy."

When Liz mentioned this, I noticed that she was walking behind me.

"Don't lag back."

"The Saudi culture book mentioned that the wife normally walks behind the husband."

I looked around and didn't notice anyone doing the same and pointed this out to Liz.

"This is not the time and place for feminist shows of strength. Let's just get to the clothing store," Liz shot back.

I must admit that it was felt weird, and for a moment, I imagined that this was what my ancestors had to do. Many theologians seemed to believe that Islam in Saudi was reminiscent of Christianity in the Middle Ages. This was an oversimplification, but Liz walking behind me as if she was property of mine was unsettling and an unwanted paradigm shift.

We arrived at the store and to Liz's surprise, she found a couple of garments that were perfect.

"I went through living a year in Korea finding one, maybe two items of clothing that fit me. First day, and score!"

"Yeah, that was hilarious. I had to buy an XXL winter, down feather jacket, which fit like a L size normally."

"Well, I think we ventured out enough for the time being. Let's go home and finish off the falafels and see if we can get the internet. I'm sure the bell-hop at the apartment might know something," I suggested.

Fortunately, we discovered that the apartment did provide free Wi-Fi, and with the password in hand, we hastily checked our email and got in contact with friends and family. All were relieved to hear that we had arrived safely.

Our bodies were still adjusting to the new time zone, and by 8pm, we went to bed. About fifteen minutes later, there was banging on the door, and once again, we were startled out of bed.

"Did the night fly by so quickly?" Liz said in an urgent voice. I shrugged my shoulders wondering if time was something that was not adhered to in Saudi and checked the keyhole. It was the driver from the morning.

"I thought you said you are coming tomorrow...?" I inquired.

"We go now to new apartment," he replied. "Bring bags and everything. No come back."

I broke the news to Liz, and she put her head under her pillow and screamed. Thankfully, her banshee shrill was not heard by anyone else, and we dutifully commenced packing and transporting our bags to the minibus. The driver assured us that the journey to the new apartment was short.

Gina joined us, and we shared a quick greeting and then conversed about the confusion. "I was told that we were leaving yesterday, so I've just been waiting..." reiterated Gina. "I have been so ready to go. The couch made me itchy. Hopefully, our new place is close to a pharmacy, since I have hives up and down my legs. Let's hope it's not bedbugs or, worse, lice."

Liz mentioned that Gina could be rest assured that it was not scabies as they had an incubation period of 2 weeks. Gina inquired as to how Liz knew that information.

Liz, without missing a beat, continued, "Alex and I love travelling, but we generally have a tight budget. On our trips to Korea, China and Japan, we stayed at backpacker lodges that were considerably cheaper, but clean. After we came back from teaching adventures in the Far East, we decided to visit a friend in Indianapolis, and without hesitation, we booked a backpacker lodge."

Liz paused for a moment and gave a shudder, remembering. "When we arrived at the lodge, we quickly realized that lodge culture in the States is completely different from what we were accustomed to. The place seemed like an inexpensive lodging option for the homeless and truckers. Suffice to say, two weeks later, we both had scabies. The itch was unbearable. Never again."

Liz told her story with horror on her face, as if she was still in that situation and concluded her story just as the minibus arrived at our new apartment. Gina, Liz and I all looked at each other with a mixture of excitement and uncertainty before we got ready to exit the vehicle. Regardless of what awaited us, this we knew: Our next chapter of this adventure was definitely not going to be boring.

CHAPTER 3
Letters from Liz, #1

Hello, everyone!

Sorry we have been so late sending you all an update from Saudi Arabia. Our internet has been on the fritz, and since it is currently oscillating around the room, I thought I'd give ya'll an update.

Well, as most of you know, we arrived safely in Saudi Arabia on November 30. I couldn't believe how COLD it was (about 48 degrees). A torrential rainstorm had just flooded parts of the highway and local roads in Riyadh. The drainage system isn't the best in Saudi, since it rains around 3 times a year.

I remember being jerked to and fro while our driver was trying to dodge puddles of water and oncoming traffic. (Saudi drivers are extremely aggressive; if I come back with high blood pressure, I'll blame it on the traffic.)

We made it safely to our "home" around 3am, and we were quickly moved again in the next few days to our permanent place.

***Perks: Aside from having a nice foyer, it's nice having an attractive entrance that also converts into a laundry drying space.

***The bathroom is awesome! We get a bathtub (a rarity in Saudi)! Most of the other residents have their shower literally on top of the toilet. We are lucky; we have our own, self-contained, bathing space! Yippee!

***The kitchen is interesting... Not a ton of counter space, but we make it work. In the front left corner of the photo is our one-and-only, genuine, plastic, Saudi-made washing machine and spinner. This washer is filled using that little faucet at the kitchen sink. Once filled, we watch in wonder while the washer utilizes "the punch" system to clean our clothes. Basically, the "punch system" is a long, plastic rod that randomly punches up and entangles our beautiful fabrics with one another. So far, we've found that this revolutionary "punch system" not only entangles but creates small holes in our clothing too. LOL

***Finally, the shining glory of this place is the flat screen T.V. We get 200 channels of which about 5 of them speak English! That's more English-speaking channels then we ever had in Michigan! (We never had cable and only got 3 PBS channels.) Plus, this awesome television set comes equipped with a USB port, so we can download and watch our favorite movies/shows on our 37-inch big screen, instead of huddled around the computer. Very cool.

I've been surprised at how different Saudi Arabia has been compared to my expectations. I thought it would be an extremely conservative and uptight place. So far, I've noticed: The university buildings are gorgeous and state of the art. The students lack motivation, and things are gloriously disorganized at work! It makes every day an adventure. So far, I've learned while in Saudi: You need to be flexible, patient, and always put a positive spin on things. I will get into the work environment a bit more in my next email... because, currently, I AM ON A PAID VACATION! Yes, it's true. School is out for the semester and I'm currently being paid to be on vacation for the past week and next few days. I'd much rather talk about vacation experiences and leave work as next month's email topic.

Things I've done and learned over vacation:

Saudi Arabia is conservative, but not as conservative as I expected—especially outside of Riyadh. Let me elaborate on that point. Since arriving in Saudi Arabia, all the stories and culture shock books I've read have been worst-case scenarios, with every topic considered slightly taboo. For example, the *Culture Shock Saudi Arabia* instructed us, "Don't bring in medicine from another country, it will be confiscated! Oh, and don't even think of bringing your computers because you'll be stuck at customs for hours on end, while they go through every single file!" Pretty scary huh? I was absolutely frightened that our wedding pictures on our computer might be considered scandalous because I was wearing a strapless dress! Ha, ha!

But, the reality of Riyadh is the work acumen is not the best by a long shot, and the airport security can't be bothered with searching for anything—especially computers. Granted it was 3am in the morning, and the guy that was supposed to be watching the baggage camera that we put our bags through was sleeping! We got through customs without ever opening our bag and breezed through the rest in about 15 minutes. Victory! I got to keep our wedding pictures and our medicine!

Call to Prayer - I remember once in a Bible class, we were chatting about Islam, and a congregant said, "I just don't understand how they can hold down a job and pray 5 times a day." I just want to take this moment to give that person credit where credit is due. I have no idea how businesses survive here. They have call to prayer at the most random times. I want to eat dinner, but I can't because someone is singing over a loud speaker, and all the restaurants are closed. Okay... what? All this nonsense makes me keen on staying home and cooking to the tune of the "Takbir", whilst smiling to myself that I am the one and only person being productive for the next hour.

Riyadh is very strict about the call to prayer. They have these guys called the *Mutaween*, or the religious police that basically make sure people go to prayer when the call is being sung via the loud speaker. They have tried to corral Alex into following them to the mosque on several occasions. It is always an interesting debate to watch. The *Mutaween* are very strong in Riyadh, but their power is not as strong in other parts of Saudi Arabia.

When I was enjoying part of my paid vacation in Khobar (East Coast of Saudi, near the bridge to Bahrain), I noticed a few *Mutaween* at the mall being ignored and even laughed at by some of the men during the call to prayer. Less than half of the men bothered to get up and go to the mosque. The other half ignored the chanting, while chatting with each other over dinner.

That is very different from Riyadh. Not only do we wake up to this loudspeaker singer (who doesn't always have an excellent singing voice, by the way) at around 5am and again around 6am, but we get to look forward to it singing us to sleep as well. It is the most "interesting" happening to have your shopping, your dinner, or your conversation interrupted with a loud announcement that the call to prayer will be starting shortly. I used to dislike this announcement, kicking my feet at the dust, wondering how I would spend my time for the next 30-45 minutes while the whole city shut down... but now I plan my restaurant meals and coffee breaks around it.

When I hear the loudspeaker announcement that the call to prayer is starting, Alex and I immediately rev our engines and start sprinting to the nearest Starbucks to get our latte and a free Wi-Fi hotspot. It's much better to sip on some caffeine and read the news or our emails then stand outside a locked building in the hot sun. Sometimes, there is no way around being locked out, but then again, I guess that's because I have to get better at striding fast in my *abaya.*

Required Attire - Okay, the following are only Riyadh attire rules. I've heard rumors that things are different in Jeddah (a somewhat more liberal Saudi city, located on the West Coast of The Kingdom). I have not been there, though, so I cannot attest to whether they bend the rules about Saudi attire or not. However, myth has it that women in Jeddah can wear their *abaya* OPEN ((gasp!)), like a long cardigan. Some of them even show their knees!! Also, I heard Jeddah women can experiment with colorful *abayas* and *hijabs*. Finally, I heard women can wear normal one-piece bathing suits, and don't have to wear their modest swimwear.

Basically, men can wear whatever they want. Alex is welcome to wear western clothes to work (as long as it's not obscene, like biker spandex shorts), or he can choose to wear the traditional Saudi wear, known as a *thobe*, which is basically a long, white garment that the guys wear with a red, checked scarf head covering known as the *keffiyeh.* These guys take their *thobe* wear very seriously and have top designers like Versace make their white dress, overtop, cotton, long underwear as stylish as humanly possible.

As for me, I have to wear the *abaya* (a black, loose-fitting cloak that covers my body like a long jacket that goes to my wrists and ankles) and a *hijab* (basically a scarf that covers my hair and neck). In Riyadh, I believe it is required that I wear a black *abaya* only. However, if I'm feeling a little risky, I can opt for a colorful head scarf (which I usually do). Some of my colleagues opt for no scarf at all and usually walk away unscathed, but they are definitely serviced with disapproving stares and remarks. I don't mind wearing the headscarf, because I'm just thankful that I don't have to wear the *niqab* that all the Saudi women tend to wear. The *niqab* is a veil that tends to make the women look like they are ninjas. It has eye holes, and it ties behind their head, just like a real live ninja. Every time I see them, I wonder if they have some crazy kung fu moves or a round-house kick to die for.

Anyway, now that I've officially bored you with some basics of the culture, I would appreciate your thoughts and prayers while Alex and I continue adjusting to this new culture. I have a request that you especially pray for our safety on the roads. Like I said before, Saudi drivers are very aggressive. One of the teachers that I know was paralyzed after her bus got into a serious accident. That was over a year ago. Since then, she has regained her ability to walk, but still has to go to physical therapy every week. So, we'd really appreciate your thoughts with us in that area.

Also, please remember to pray for us to remain patient, loving, and kind to our colleagues and students. Since we obviously can't always express what we want to share in words, we hope for guidance in showing love through our actions.

I will try to send another update next month highlighting our work and some of the local Saudi cuisine. So exciting!!

Peace,
Liz

CHAPTER 4
Not in Michigan Anymore

The first days in our new apartment were marked with a blend of sleep to correct our jetlag and gentle exploration of our immediate vicinity. We quickly realized that besides a small shop providing the bare essentials, our area was devoid of any other means of spending our oil money. Most food restaurants and takeaways were at least a mile away, and in Saudi terms, that was far. Even though it was winter, during the day, the piercing sun felt as if it was stabbing our skin, and most of the streets did not have any sidewalks.

Liz had to wear the _abaya_, which was basically a full black dress that covered her arms, legs and all of her skin besides her face. Her hair had to be covered by a _hijab_, as any show of hair was seen as disrespectful. The Turkish woman in the mini taxi all those days ago mentioned that for every hair that was visible, a saint was sobbing. Liz probably brought the entire pantheon of saints and future ones, as well, to uncontrollable wailing. As she was unfamiliar with putting on the *hijab*, she could never get every strand of hair to cooperate.

We decided to take the plunge and hail the first taxi to come by and say one word: "Mall". Like most trips in a taxi, when one does not know their destination, the trip, no matter how close, usually takes long. We used a tall building in the distance as a marker and found ourselves going around it a few times in looping slow-motion, reminiscent of a moth to a candle flame. All the while, the meter continued to tick merrily along.

In South Korea, we made a game of looking for English advertisements alongside the road that were lost in translation. We came across many gems in Korea. Five minutes into our Saudi drive, we were not disappointed. "Organ donation. The climax of giving." Classic!

About thirty minutes later, we arrived at the mall, with an inflated meter and serious concerns that we were taken for a ride at our expense. It seemed that a taxi driver's love for the open road and taking pride in enjoying his drive for an unspecified duration knew no boundaries. Having travelled extensively, this mindset transcended nationality, race and creed. I suspected that every new taxi driver's initiative was given the secret book of how to enjoy your profession with long Sunday drives, whereby the straightest line is never the best path.

Liz looked at me, with her eyes wide and mouth agape with horror. Do we negotiate, or do we risk prison by protesting? Could it come to the latter? It could be considered theft if we underpay, I hypothesized. Pay him, I did, but I realized that just because everyone was running off to mosque 5 times a day, in what is considered the most religious country in the world, honesty in the taxi driver industry remained on par with the rest of the world. This was an expensive lesson, and I realized that I would have to find out how the locals addressed the dreaded taxi driver. I was told that Saudi was one of the cheapest cities in the world, and I had just paid New York cab prices.

Since this was the first time we had some downtime, we decided to walk around before entering the mall. We found it interesting that sidewalks would just end on busy streets, and besides the masses of vehicles, there was not many people on the street. Downtown Riyadh did not seem like a city that encouraged much walking.

People were concentrated around malls and restaurants. After the sidewalk ended abruptly at a busy intersection, we turned around and took a good look at the mall. It was called Panorama, and it seemed like a mid-sized mall with the usual stores, which went a long way in making us comfortable. We walked around the mall in a grid-like fashion, hoping to see every store they had to offer.

The mall was anchored by a large, chain supermarket called Panda. The store logo was literally a panda bear. Having a supermarket in a mall was something I had never seen back home, and I think we missed a trick on that. The mall was truly our one stop shop, and in a foreign land, this was a relief and one less thing to worry about.

While walking around the mall, we noticed a difference almost immediately. The local men wore the traditional Saudi *thobe*, and women wore full black body *abayas*, a *niquab* covering everything but their eyes, and most wore black gloves to cover the hands. On the other hand, a foreigner could be spotted a mile away. The men wore western clothing, and the ladies, while wearing an *abaya*, did not cover their hair at all.

"Risky," Liz commented and proceeded to take her head scarf off. "When in Rome...?"

Her female empowerment lasted all but ten minutes. While walking boldly at the center atrium of the mall, I felt someone tap me on the shoulder. I looked around, and I saw a man in an ornately decorated *thobe* lined with gold thread and young cadet at his side.

I asked him how I could be of assistance, and he went straight into explaining to us that in his country, women cover their hair. In a quick fashion, accentuated with fear, Liz threw her head scarf on. Back to reality. We hastily retreated into the closest store and shared a couple of deep breaths. We decided to end our aimless walking and went straight into the supermarket. After procuring some groceries and a few pots and pans for our new apartment, we headed back into the sun, wondering how exactly we would get home.

I had taken a business card from the apartment's front desk, and it did show the street of our apartment, but nothing else. Road names were rarely displayed. Additionally, our area was a new development, so I had little to no faith the taxi driver would find the place. Thankfully, the business card also had a number for the guy at the front desk whom I had yet to acquaint myself with.

After jumping in a taxi, we gave the driver the universal sign of "just a minute" by holding up a finger and slightly moving it back and forth in a vigorous fashion. After 10 rings and almost giving up, the phone was answered, and I quickly gave it to the confused driver, who listened to the front desk guy give him instructions.

The taxi driver chanted, "Apartment, apartment..." over and over again before hanging up and handing me back the phone. By the nodding of the driver's head, it seemed as if was we were in the clear, and I felt relieved.

This was short-lived, however, as the driver went down several streets, abruptly stopped and did many u-turns. I wasn't sure if he was running the meter or was genuinely lost. I eventually suspected the former. After driving around "lost" in the city for 15 minutes, we went on a main highway that surprisingly took us straight to our apartment, minus two or three turns after getting off the highway.

The second trip helped me to get a bearing on

the directions to downtown, and I would be more questioning the next time. Even with all the time wasting in the city, our taxi ride was twenty dollars cheaper than the first trip and significantly quicker.

Walking into the entrance of the apartment, we saw in the corner was a desk and man, who I presumed to be the person who directed the taxi driver earlier.

"Hi, I'm Alex, and this is Liz. We moved in yesterday."

"Hi, I'm Abdul. I work at here at front desk. Did you call for directions earlier?"

"Yes, thank you for helping us. We were so worried. I'm so relieved that you pointed us in the right direction."

"Any time problem, call. Food, taxi, anything. You call, I help."

"Thanks again," I replied.

Liz and I turned to go to our apartment, but then I remembered, "Oh, Abdul, is there a place to do shopping other than the mall downtown?"

"Yes, Mr. Alex. A mall near, near."

Abdul pointed back and forth to indicate the direction of the (as we would later find out) much closer mall. It was in the opposite direction of the other mall. That was the final embarrassment associated with the trip, and I vowed never to be an ignorant expat again.

The next day would be our first day at our

respective universities. We were informed by Osmah that there were two teaching shifts: 7am to 3pm and 9am to 5pm. Since we did not have any class assignments yet, we were told to take the company provided shuttle for one of those shifts to the university.

Naturally, with all our nervous enthusiasm, we chose the early shuttle. Liz and I parted ways at the entrance of the apartment building and promised to share every detail when we got home.

The shuttle bus came promptly at 6:30am, and a weary group of men slowly shuffled on to the shuttle. It had the distinct impression of a funeral procession.

Liz and I had accepted the teaching jobs out of the regular hiring period and had arrived a month before the end of the first semester as replacements for those who had left prior to the end of their contracts. When I first heard of this phenomenon, the first thing I thought of was the movie *Midnight Run*—trying to get out an unfavorable situation in the Middle East without raising the slightest alarm.

In the next couple of weeks, I would use that term quite often in reference to people who threw their bags out of windows in the middle of the night, so as not to raise the alarm with the front desk attendant who, I was told, was instructed to report any person leaving the apartment with suitcases to the company. Surprisingly it caught on and became the officially accepted term amongst my fellow peers for an overnight exit from Saudi.

We had arrived in the middle of winter, so the daylight hours were reduced. I'm not sure if the darkness combined with the end of the semester was to blame, but most people on the shuttle looked depressed. I struck a conversation with the person sitting next to me, first exchanging pleasantries. Sath was a first-generation British Pakistani who had found it difficult to find a job in England, so he opted to teach in The Kingdom and get a religious experience at the same time.

He discussed the high turnover of teachers and the remaining teachers being given the option of teaching extra classes for 50% of their normal compensation. Some who desperately needed the money gladly accepted the extra work, while others scoffed at the idea of being worked to death for half the pay. He fell under the former group, and as a married man with young kids and a young wife, halfway across the world, he felt he had no choice in the matter.

This was a sobering conversation, and I looked around and realized that many of the men I shared this shuttle with had not seen their wives, children and families in six months, and I felt a little guilty that I had my wife with me to confide in and share my thoughts and feelings with on this journey.

Thirty minutes later, the shuttle dropped us off at the university. The building was huge, square and painted light brown, which incidentally made it blend into its dusty surroundings. Sath pointed out that the building was painted white a few months ago, and the continuous dust storms turned it into its current shade of tan.

Upon inquiry, a few of my fellow travelers in the shuttle directed me to the HR officer's room, which I would have never found if left to my own devices. The building was set up like a maze with many corridors and alleys, leading to who knows where. Even though I was given detailed instructions, I lost my way and had to ask for assistance.

The HR officer's room was literally at the furthest point from the entrance of the university, on the top fourth floor. It seemed as if it was purposefully put there to make sure the officer did not get inundated with workers at any given time.

I knocked on the door, and there was no answer. I waited a minute then I knocked again with greater gusto. Nothing. I walked along the corridor, trying to find anyone in the office, but it was a ghost town. I stood outside the HR room for about 20 minutes, until someone finally entered an office at the end of the corridor.

I briskly walked over, hoping for some answers.

"Ah, you are looking for Ahmed. He only comes in at 9am," the man replied.

I thanked him and decided to explore the university with the one hour and thirty minutes I now had to waste.

On the ground floor, there was a central atrium

with a food court. I did not have breakfast, so I perused my options. Pizza, burgers, falafel wraps, roasted chicken, fried fish, freshly squeezed juice, tea and sweet cakes. They had a great selection. I walked towards the rear exit of the building and happened upon a street that had over ten restaurants and a large, world-class gym. Things were looking up, and I could see the potential for having great food and even better workouts during my downtime.

I made my way back to the university and meandered to the fourth floor. The HR office was open, and there were other men, likely new recruits, sitting in the office. I knocked on the door, inquiring if I was in the right spot and took the only remaining seat.

We were asked to give a brief description of our past teaching experiences. After that, we were given a tour of the college, which felt like the movie *Groundhog Day*, but we did swing past the library, which I had not found earlier.

The library was small, but a welcome retreat from the hustle and bustle of the other common areas. We were also shown the prayer areas around the campus, if we were ever compelled to worship. The group of guys that started with me were a mix of first-generation Muslims living in Britain, Canada and the U.S.A., primarily with heritage from Pakistan, Sudan and Afghanistan. The next set of recruits were Christian and atheist old men around 40 to 65 years of age from Australia, U.S.A.

and Britain, who lost their jobs in the financial crash of the late 2000's.

The guy I sat next to during the orientation was named Rex, from England, and he seemed more at ease than the rest of us. During our lunch break, he mentioned that this was his third time coming to work in Saudi but the first time working for this education company. I was under the impression that we were employed by the government, but he quickly set me straight.

"In Saudi, nobody wants to accept responsibility for any mistakes or problems that may arise, especially in a government-sponsored workplace —probably a cultural face-saving mechanism. The university subcontracts the hiring and firing of teachers to independent sourcing companies. Whenever a problem arises that cannot be swept under the carpet, the company is blamed, penalized or fired, and the whole process resets. It really doesn't matter too much in the end as this university is an English preparatory institute with a prime function of keeping young men off the streets and out of trouble."

"What do you mean exactly?"

It was only the two of us sitting together, but Rex looked around quickly to see if anyone else was near and listening. He leaned in close. "The walls have ears. Be careful what you say and repeat. People have been fired for conversations that may seem mundane to you. Any talk that puts Saudi in a negative light can be misconstrued as sedition, and they don't waste time firing teachers. This place is a revolving door, with a turnover of over 70% from semester to semester. They know that there are plenty more desperate souls like me and you willing to fill the void."

"That explains the large number of new teachers," I remarked.

"Yes, it is a weekly occurrence. You will notice it soon enough. Once a group of teachers decided to protest longer working hours and were dismissed on the spot as the recruiter deemed their actions as unionization. Unions of any kind are banned. Getting an actual college education is just for show. They don't really care if the students fail or pass.

"The students are paid a living stipend for attending, which is more than what that cleaner, sweeping the floor, earns in a month. They realize that most of the students will never amount to much, but they still use this place as a way to prevent an Arab Spring, or political protests, in Saudi. I would say that 80 to 90 percent of all the jobs in Saudi are done by foreigners."

As he spoke, certain things started to click in my head. I noticed that most of the people who worked in store fronts were not Saudis, and taking stock of this, I noticed that the college was run by foreigners. The only Saudi who "worked" there was the dean of the university, and Rex indicated that no one had ever seen him in his office. It was last heard that he was in England with a soccer season pass in hand.

"Saudi is an interesting place for all the wrong reasons," Rex continued. "Before oil was discovered, Saudis were dirt poor and lived a pastoral, Bedouin lifestyle. Slavery was legal, and slaves did most, if not all, of the chores around the camp. In fact, slavery was only abolished in the sixties at the insistence of Kennedy.

"After oil was discovered, cities grew rapidly, but besides menial labor from slaves, there wasn't anyone to perform professional services, such as doctors, engineers and so forth. Saudi imported the labor, and so it has remained.

"The slave/master mindset runs deep in the psyche of Saudis. They see you as a person performing a task at their bequest. Recently, there has been a push for 'Saudization', whereby the government wants to employ more Saudis, but they face stiff opposition from business owners who are, by and large, Saudis.

"Saudization hopes to fill the professional jobs taken by foreigners, but there is a small problem: Saudi culture. Work ethic is not part of Saudi culture, so if a company employs a Saudi, they also need to employ another person: a foreigner to actually do the job. If you employ a Saudi, they can never be fired. That does not bode well for businesses that are profit-motivated. You basically have a passenger who is earning a top salary.

"And, remember, businesses close for the call to pray at least 3 times during working hours and

5 times total every day. I have heard business owners complain that their Saudi workers go to the mosque and return hours later on a trip that usually takes 10 to 15 minutes at the most, just in time for the next call to pray. Saudi law dictates that there should be a mosque every 500 meters, so it should not take that long."

I felt like my head was going to explode with all this information. Our lunch hour was almost up, and we decided to head back to the HR office. On a parting note, Rex told me to be careful with whom I trusted and talked to, and he mentioned that people are polarized.

"While this is not everyone, beware of the foreigners who come to Saudi for a religious experience. They tend to become empowered here and report anything out of the ordinary to the religious police. A few years ago, my apartment block wanted to have a Christmas Secret Santa, but we were reported to the police by a colleague and fellow countryman."

Rex's final thought left me a little unsettled. It seemed like there was more going on here than what met the eye, but I was not going to treat anyone differently based on his or her race, religion or heritage. I reasoned that if I was respectful to everyone and sensitive in conversation, mutual respect would prevail.

We went back to the HR office and were told that we were done for the day and that we could get adjusted to our surroundings while waiting for the shuttle to arrive in two hours. Since Rex and I had conversed throughout our lunch hour, we joined the new recruits for a snack at a Syrian restaurant next to the university.

The food was excellent, consisting of flat breads, baked in a pizza oven with various toppings of your choice. I tried a labneh (a Middle Eastern yogurt) with a Middle Eastern, spice-mix topping. simple yet delicious. I could not wait to try the different toppings over the next few months.

After ordering our food, we went around the table introducing ourselves. After the brief introductions, individual conversations broke out as if the nervousness of the first day had finally abated. I could hear a little from each conversation, talk of family, citizenship and elaborations about how they found themselves in Saudi.

The person sitting next to me who had earlier introduced himself as Duncan from Ireland interrupted my eavesdropping with a question. I felt bad that I hadn't been paying attention to him. "Duncan, right? I'm so sorry. I didn't quite catch your question."

"I'm told that there are generally three reasons why anyone comes to Saudi: for the religious experience, professional or monetary gain, or running away from something.

What category do you fit into?" Duncan asked.

I gave a little chuckle at how true his statement was. "Definitely the second one, specifically the money aspect. Granted my dream job is to be a university professor, and this fulfils a life dream. However, this is not exactly the place I would have liked my dream to be realized. But, at this point in my life, I will take it."

"Pretty much the same for me, well the money part that is," Duncan shared. "Once Ireland's economy collapsed in the late 2000's, I lost my job almost immediately. I have been coming to Saudi off and on for the last 2 years. Hopefully, Ireland picks up, because I have had my fill of this place. But on the flip side, nowhere else pays more for 4 hours of work, especially since I have a non-education-related master's degree. I think it is important to send a check home to the wife and kids. While I miss them, I just have to do what is best for them, you know?"

On the way home on the shuttle, I stared out of the window, lost in thought, contemplating all that was said. I felt almost out of my depth in most regards. Most of the teachers had years of experience and had a graduate degree. There also seemed to be an undercurrent of animosity between teachers that I had barely begun to scrape the surface of, and the stark, light brown landscape did nothing to improve my mood.

Feeling a little jaded, I arrived at our apartment to find Liz energetically cleaning the apartment. After we greeted each other Liz chatted on, even though I was still lost in my thoughts. "The dust hasn't even settled, and I have been given a class. The women's university is understaffed and desperate for teachers. They have even more Saudi ladies that have been given classes, as well, that don't have a degree, but they do have a proficiency in English. It's terrible what the powers that be are doing. They are paid half of my salary. This will only lead to bitterness and resentment. I know I would be upset if the shoe was on the other foot."

She nudged me to make sure I was paying attention, as she changed the subject. "Anyway, I was told that we live about 10 minutes from a large mall. We need to go there as soon as possible. Eat, shop, explore… I'm told by a few of the ladies that it is important to get a cab driver you can rely on and can call when you need transport. I will leave that to you. I'm sure Abdul will have some leads. Anyway, how was your day?"

After briefly going over my day, we left our apartment and were fortunate to see a taxi dropping off another resident/teacher, thus becoming available just for us. We eased into the taxi and told the driver our destination. Hoping that this may be "our guy", I asked him where he was from and his name, which was "Noauf", and we made a little small talk before asking if he could pick us up regularly if we called him directly. He readily agreed, and we exchanged phone numbers and input them into our phones.

Noauf continuously nodded his head, while speaking. "I'm from Jeddah in the east, and I came to Riyadh for a job. No job. I studied pharmacy but have not found a job. I asked the King for help. No help. I have a lady I want to marry, but I can't. No money and no job. All pharmacy jobs are run by foreigners, and no one wants to hire me. I have no money to start my own business, so I have to be taxi driver."

All of a sudden, I was transported to a conversation I had with Ryan, a friend of mine, while teaching in South Korea. "Sex! That's what it all comes down to. Having a whole generation of sexually frustrated men can and has led to revolutions. That's my take on the Arab Spring. Simplistic, but on point," said Ryan.

Ryan and I had followed the Arab Spring sweeping across North Africa and the Middle East with much interest in 2009. We empathized with the current situation that the youth in these countries faced, as we had left our countries because we could not find a job. I felt sad for Noauf as, unlike us, he did not have an overseas job waiting for him, based on his native language. Even with a degree in the medical field, which most seemed to think was a guaranteed path to a job, he felt his future was bleak and had resigned himself to driving a taxi.

I wondered if there was an Arab Spring on the cards for Arabians. Surely, this way of life could not be maintained. I decided then and there that I would ask Noauf to be our personal driver and made sure to pay him over and above the required amount. His story touched my heart and humanized the country for the first time since we arrived.

The mall was a ten-minute drive and was large with all the amenities we needed. We decided to check out the food court before we were sucked into aimless window shopping and discovered a vast array of Indian, Persian, Italian, Turkish and fast food fare, all under one roof.

After a quick walk through the food court, we decided on a Turkish restaurant. Liz had the falafels with hummus and grape leaves, while I had a chicken shish kebab with bulgur rice on the side. The food was delicious, and we knew that we had found our regular place.

Walking off our food in the mall, we realized that the double story mall, which was shaped like a rectangle, would be the perfect air-conditioned workout arena. Since the streets hardly had sidewalks, and the drivers tended to speed and attempted drifting techniques on suburban roads, it was best to get our walking exercise in the safety and comfort of the mall.

While walking in the mall, we walked past the guy that had mentioned he was "Philly, born and raised". He was walking with other *thobe*-wearing guys who were from the Nation of Islam table. We exchanged nods, and that was the last time I saw him.

Liz commented that guys sitting around doing

nothing scandal more than a group of ladies. I seemed to think that the scandal talk was on par, but over the course of the first few weeks, I seemed to have more crazy stories than Liz, thus cementing her views. Through the grapevine, which is how most news spread, we heard that "Philly" had done a midnight run and was now teaching in Turkey. Go figure.

Over the next few days, the group of new recruits, at King Saud University (the Men's University), began to whittle down, as people found groups that shared their citizenship, faith or heritage. Before long, I lifted my head one day after taking a sip of tea and felt like I was in high school all over again. The African American Nation of Islam group sat in one corner, Sudanese-heritage Muslims hung out in another corner and the Pakistani-heritage Muslims occupied a space somewhere in the middle. Hovering all around were the "nomads" that were not religiously affiliated.

All religions besides Islam were banned in Saudi, so religious talk among non-Muslims was kept to a bare minimum. I formed a group with the non-religious new recruits (more accurately the "religion not to be discussed" group) and became friends with many others who fell into this group. While it wasn't ideal, it was the easiest thing to do.

We taught for four hours, but we were contracted to stay on campus for 8 hours altogether.

This led to a lot of downtime and boredom. Since I was not assigned a class for the time being, I had 8 hours to kill. There was only so much a person could do on their computer, so I found myself walking around and observing the students praying in the allocated areas and asking questions about Islam to my Muslim acquaintances.

One thing they all agreed *on* and made mention of was that Islam was perfect in every way, and the Quran did not have any contradictions. A quick Google search put the latter claim to rest, but with the nature of the country, I did not bring it up.

Rex had retreated to a newly-vacated office, only to be seen a few times again, but he did leave a lasting impression on me. I felt ignorant and did not want to get sucked into prejudicial thinking. Knowledge is power, and I hoped to empower myself. I firmly believed that understanding built bridges, especially when humans had a tendency to have a default setting of looking upon different racial groups, religions and many other tags with suspicion. I was determined to learn more about Islam in Saudi.

A few days later, during my lunch period, I noticed Sath sitting alone. Up until now, he had been one of the only people that spoke to me candidly about Islam. Since he came to Saudi for a job and a religious experience, he would be in a better position than most books I could find on the subject at Saudi bookstores. He was more than happy to share his understanding of Islam in the hopes that it would allow me to navigate the country and the students with a better understanding and sensitivity. He also felt that if I listened with an open mind and heart, I would see no reason not to accept the prophet Mohamed as the last testament of God, or at least begin my journey to becoming, as he put it, "one who submits to the will of God", which is what the word Muslim means.

"First off, Islam preaches that all Muslims are equal. In a perfect world, we all should be equal. But people are people and prejudices can get in the way. That is the sinful nature of this world. For example, I wanted a visa for my wife, but when filling out the necessary documents, the Saudi immigration officer asked me my citizenship. I told him English, and he shook his head and said, 'No, I'm talking about were your heritage is from.'

"Thinking nothing of it, I said, 'Pakistan.' Instantly, he put a rejection stamp on my application. There is discrimination in the Middle East, especially amongst the rich countries towards the poorer ones. Even Islam, at times, cannot escape economic and regional classism that is prevalent around the world. The whole notion of having a King flies in the face of Islamic doctrine. It creates a social stratification that the Prophet preached against."

While Sath spoke about his desire to have equality in his religion and also the world, I thought about what he said about the creation of Islam. There always seemed to be a pecking order. This could be said about any religion or government. Democratic governments are seen as a government "by the people and for the people", but how often do we see the government employees receive preferential treatment over the rest of the populous? This was not even discussing office abuse of power but benefits, such as lifetime salaries, pensions, medical and so forth.

Just because someone represented a community, it does not give them the right to have benefits that no one else is privy to. Even in democracy, there is social stratification. Are we, as humans, programmed to create systems of classism and, in turn, could it be argued that is part of the human condition? I felt myself recalling similar conversations that I had at college amongst my peers in sociology—discussions of equality, unity and the occasional existentialism detour.

Sath continued, "Islam has its roots long before the Prophet Mohammed (peace be upon him). We say 'peace be upon him' as a mark of respect and reverence to prophets sent from God. Just like Judaism and Christianity, Islam is an Abrahamic religion. Meaning it was based and founded by the covenant between God and Abraham.

"We believe in all the prophets of the Bible and consider Jesus a prophet, but not the Son of God. The Bible is the Word of God, and we consider it true. Mohammed is the last prophet sent from

God, and the Quran is seen as the last testament of God's commandments, grace and benevolence on his people. Stop me at any time if you have questions."

"Yeah, I do have a question, I said. "I'm curious to know why Jesus is not seen as the Son of God? If the Bible is considered to be God's Word and true, wouldn't it be true to say that Jesus is the Son of God as claimed in the Bible?"

Sath continued, "Well, we do view the Quran as the final word of God and whatever is said in the Quran takes precedence over earlier writings. According to Islam, Jesus was believed to have been taken up to Heaven, like the prophet Elijah. He did not physically die, but he was alive and raised up to Heaven. Jesus is seen as a prophet, and it is believed that Jesus will be sent back to us to defeat the Al Mashih Ad Dajjal, which is called the anti-Christ in Christianity.

"Just like Jerusalem is the center of Judaism, Mecca is considered the holiest city in Islam. As believers, we are compelled to follow and actively practice the Five Pillars of Islam. The first two are Shadahah, which is the declaration of faith, and Salat, which obliges Muslims to pray five times a day. I'm sure you have noticed that all business comes to a halt when you hear the call to pray.

"Ideally, businesses should be closed for 5 to 15 minutes, but many take advantage of this time and report back to work, sometimes over an hour later. One prayer is early in the morning, so this does not affect business. The last four can impact the day-to-day business. Also, if you noticed, the class periods are aligned with the prayer times, so our periods are different than what you are accustomed to. With the extra time away from class during the middle session, I don't see too many people complaining.

"The third pillar is Zakat, which is giving alms to the poor. The fourth is fasting during Ramadan. The third and fourth pillar then to go hand-in-hand. Ramadan can be seen as an empathy exercise, whereby we understand what it feels like to be poor and hungry. During Ramadan, Muslims fast from sun up to sun down. Now non-Muslims in Saudi are not obligated to observe Ramadan, but I advise you to eat in private, as some people can become irate if they see others not following Ramadan."

"That is interesting," I interjected. "People can get angry for seeing others eat? Would the exercise of seeing others eat while you are hungry give someone a more accurate feeling of what it is like to be poor and hungry?"

Sath nodded and explained, "While I do agree with that, it must be understood that Saudi is a Muslim majority country, and the worship of other religions is banned. So, most Saudis consider everyone in Saudi to be Muslims, whether they like it or not. If they see you eating, they see it as sacrilegious.

"In Saudi, there are two types of police: the

normal police and the religious police. The religious police, called the *Mutaween*, believe that it is their job to be the upholders of virtue and the prevention of vice. You mentioned that you met one in the mall a few weeks ago, yes? The king has been reducing their powers over the last couple of months.

"Most Saudis consider themselves to be a moral compass and will call out something they see as wrong. Foreigners often have parties broken up by the *Mutaween*, who were called in by citizens. Remember that all Saudis can be the *Mutaween*, and Big Brother is always watching."

Sath and I laughed a little with his 1984 reference, but I had a sense of dread after hearing this. It was as if a paradigm shift occurred with regards to my outlook of Saudi, and I found myself clutching the book in my hand, feeling somewhat guarded and unsettled. I would definitely be more cautious when I was out in the open.

Sath continued, "The final pillar of Islam is a pilgrimage to Mecca. One of the reasons I took this job was to complete this aspect of the five pillars. I plan on going to Mecca at the end of Ramadan, which is the traditional time to go, but not necessarily the only time one can go.

"At the end of Ramadan, Eid is celebrated, and millions of people from around the world complete their pilgrimage. It's a great time of fellowship and giving. It is the closest holiday that can be compared to Christmas. There are no gifts exchanged in the traditional sense, but you do see many examples of generosity, especially to those who are less fortunate."

I asked, "I noticed that Saudi culture, religion and law seem to be intertwined. How does Sharia Law factor into the religion?"

Sath nodded. "Yes, your observations are correct. Islam is the religion and the law. The two cannot be separated, as they are one. Just like water is H2O, without either, water cannot exist. Islam also includes banking laws, which say that the charging of interest is forbidden and that the commandments in regard to the welfare of women must be followed.

"In Saudi, it is legal to marry up to four women. Most people who hear this don't quite understand the full extent of how this can be realized. If a man cannot give the same standard of living to each and every wife, then he cannot marry other wives.

"Some would also like you to think that, unlike Christianity with its many denominations, Islam is uniform throughout the world. This is not true. Within the two most recognized denominations of Sunni and Shia, there are subtle differences in religion, worship and practice, depending on the region.

"Saudi has its own flavor of Islam. Many Saudis like to think that it is the only way Islam has ever been practiced and the one, true way, but a quick study of the history of Islam in Saudi shows this not to be true. Imagine the dogmatic Christianity of the Middle Ages making a comeback today. How would it be viewed by Christians? Sure enough, some will praise it as it harkens back to a time that the Church had control of every aspect of your life, and others would merely dispel it as fundamentalism.

"In the 1800's, the Saudi king aligned himself with an ultra-conservative cleric, named Muhammad Wahhab. He called for a return to the Quran and the ways of old. This meant no form of idolatry, including visiting tombs of religious giants, including Mohammed (PBUH), and no veneration of any graven images. Wahhabism touches on every aspect of life, including the treatment of women.

"Now, most Muslim countries see this as a distortion of Islam, and these may not be out rightly denounced due to the Saudi King currying favor with goodwill donations of money for wasta, which is Arabic for 'good favor'. This goodwill has had the desired effect on obtaining a positive face for Wahhabism, and many foreigners now come to Saudi, expecting a group of people so close to the word that they are elevated on a pedestal.

"Saudis are seen by some as God's chosen people, in the same way that Jews are viewed by some as God's chosen people. God decided to reveal his last testament here in Saudi, which makes this land sacred, which creates an interesting dynamic between Saudis and some foreign Muslims coming to Saudi, looking for enlightenment and a religious experience.

"I will use myself as an example. I needed a job, but I chose Saudi specifically so that I could enrich myself, both spiritually and financially. I believed that I could learn much from the Saudis, even though I spent the better part of my life studying the Quran. What I found, like most others have discovered as well, is that the run-of-the-mill Saudi off the street is generally ignorant by western standards—ignorant about Islam and generally the world around him. The mindset is that of someone who has lived in isolation from the world and still has a mindset from the Middle Ages. While this is not everyone, it is enough people to make it noticeable. This, in turn, has an interesting effect on some foreigners Muslims who come to Saudi looking for a religious experience. They find that the 'chosen people' are not what they are thought they were, and then they feel it's their duty to show them the true way.

"Have you noticed Zahir wearing a *thobe* that is tight, above his ankles, and makes him look like a shuffling penguin?"

I smiled at the picture in my mind and said, "Yeah, great guy. We came here within a few weeks of each other."

"Have you ever wondered why his *thobe* is tight and short? Well, there is a story in the Quran of which he is trying to emulate the moral, literally. A rich man, with an elaborately designed *thobe* that was so long that it dragged on the floor, asked Mohammed how much it would cost him to attain eternal life. Mohamed shook his head and said that you cannot buy your way into heaven. You must begin with changing the way you think. Take the extra clothes you are wearing, sell it to the poor and begin a life of charity."

I remarked, "That story sounds very similar to a parable of Jesus."

Sath agreed, "It is a universal message and one that the Creator holds close. Now Zahir feels that the Saudis care about money first, and with all the oil wealth, it's hard not to come to that conclusion. So, he takes the story literally as a physical reminder to those around him of the message of Mohammed. It's almost like an 'I understand the Quran more than the chosen people' attitude. I believe we are all equal, and I don't venerate anyone. We all need to hold ourselves accountable while on the righteous path.

"We have classes soon, so I will end with this: Islam's goal is world domination. This may sound scary to an unbeliever, but Islam truly feels that it is the last testament of God, and it is the duty of every Muslim to spread the good news. Only when everyone submits to the will of God will we have peace on Earth. Personally, having seen so much hate, anger and war, I long for that day."

Liz and I quickly discovered that there were two types of expats in Saudi: those that lived in compounds, and those that did not. We fell into the latter group. A compound was a walled off residential mini-town. Most consisted of housing, shops and recreational spaces, including parks, pools and a clubhouse. The clubhouse tended to be the place of most interest to the non-compound community. If you were not living in a compound, you had to have someone who lived in the compound to vouch for you. Access was generally controlled with a few checkpoints by ex-military personnel.

In the early 2000s, a few compounds were at the receiving end of terror attacks and bombings. Safety and security were taken seriously. Some expats offered to teach dance and art on the compounds and used this as a method of gaining unrestricted access into a compound.

Liz had befriended a compound regular within the first month of arriving, and three weeks after I had come to terms with no alcohol for a year, we were off to a compound to taste their finest bathtub vintage.

On the way to the compound, I kept on thinking of something funny to say after my first sip of the mystery alcohol. I settled with, "This vintage has hints of gym class sweat and toe jam." Suffice it to say, the joke fell flat and did not have the desired effect. The alcohol did. After a drink or two and some dancing to trashy Euro techno music, we were introduced to a few people, and I struck up a conversation with one of the alcohol brewers.

My first question was: "What is the safest and

easiest type of alcohol to make?"

He pointed to my cup, which was wine. He mentioned that all I would need was a plastic trash can with an overlapping lid, grape juice, sugar and yeast. He instructed that the trash can could not leach chemicals in the wine by checking the plastic number. He indicated that he used a no. 3 type plastic. A cup of sugar for every gallon of red grape juice was need, and the grape juice needed to be preservative free, as it could kill the yeast if it was not. Finally, his instructions were to clean the trash can well, combine ingredients, leaving about a half a foot space on the top in case of frothing, and in two weeks, it would be good to go. That seemed easy enough.

As a final warning, I was told not to drink alcohol from certain compounds as some unscrupulous individuals used battery acid amongst many other noxious chemicals to speed up the fermentation process. He gave me a few off the top of his head and then just had me agree to either drink his or make my own and not trust anyone else, ever. Profits made from alcohol sales could be lucrative, so people looked to have a steady supply at the expense of the customers.

The next day, while nursing my head and bruised wallet (drinking bathtub drinks proved to be an expensive commodity), Liz and I made our way to the mall to do some much-needed grocery shopping. Alcohol was illegal in Saudi, but the ingredients to make it were not.

We never did fully explore our mall and grocery supermarket, so we carved out our Saturday (weekends did not run according to the western standard of Saturday and Sunday, but Friday and Saturday) to wander through every nook and cranny.

We started walking the mall, which was a long bi-level rectangle. We found a MM (British cheap clothing store) with a great selection of clothing, and while the men's section had a changing room to try on the clothes, the women's section did not.

After asking a store employee, we discovered that there are not female changing rooms in Saudi, and as a lady, you needed to buy the clothes, try them on at home and, if they didn't fit, you could bring them back.

After pleading with a store attendant, Liz was allowed to take the clothes to the ladies' bathroom and try them on, while I remained as collateral. After what seemed like the longest 15 minutes of my life, with images of arms getting chopped off for theft floating around my head, Liz came back and put all the clothing she found back on their racks as none fitted her the way she liked. I found work pants because my last pair that I bought from a knockoff store had split after the first wash.

Phase two, we walked over to the grocery store called Carrefour, which, I was told by a colleague, was French owned. Carrefour had a better feel than the Panda store, with many familiar items and countless new ones. Since the States is not renowned for their fresh juices, we perused the fresh juice section and discovered a vast array of juice from all over the world. The best priced juice without preservatives was called Ceres, and it was produced in South Africa. I did recall sporadically buying South African wine at an international store back home, so I felt confident that I could make a usable product.

After doing our grocery shopping, we headed to the taxi section of the mall and told the driver where to take us. True to form, the driver drove in the opposite direction. I tapped the driver's shoulder and decided to point the driver every step of the way. What really helped was I had learned the Arabic word for left (*yassar*), right (*yemeen*), straight (cedar) and straight to the end of the street (*cedar al atool*). This was one of the steps I took so we would never be taken for a ride again.

So far, it was working out well. As soon as I started directing a driver, they would generally wave their hand, indicating they knew where they were going, but more importantly, they knew that I knew where I was going.

Since we arrived at the end of the first term, we only had a few weeks of teaching, and then it was vacation. While Liz was given a class straight out the gates, I had one week of orientation, which ended up being a glorified week-long coffee break.

During the second week, I covered absent

teachers' classes, and then it was done for two weeks. On the final day, we were told that even though the students would be on vacation, the teachers would still have to come in. The shuttle ride home that afternoon was tense, with short outbursts from different sections. People still knew their place, so the outbursts were measured but bitter in the same breath.

In Korea, as teachers, we often had to sit in our offices, even though the students were on vacation, so this wasn't anything new to me. We even came up with a term for it: desk warming.

Many of the teachers who had come from Thailand were used to teaching in a tropical paradise and having ample vacation time to enjoy all the country had to offer. This was quite the converse of what they experienced, and this group took the lack of vacation and Saudi, on a whole, the hardest.

Liz was given the two weeks off, so she decided to go with some new friends on a road trip to Dammam. Dammam was on the east coast, and unlike Riyadh, the dominant Islamic sect was Shia.

After two weeks of complaints, bouts of anger and a marked increase in midnight runs, the students returned to breathe some life into the stark emptiness of the building. I was given my first official class. The students were at an elementary level of English, so I was told that I would have to come up with some innovative lesson plans.

At 9am, a group of nervous-faced eighteen-year-olds entered the room. We began with a few icebreakers to get comfortable and then went through the rules of the classroom and the university attendance policy.

At the end of the class, one of the students told me that this group had failed the previous semester due to poor attendance and they would try their best this term. The attendance policy was generous. The students were allowed 30 excused days per semester. That worked out to half the semester excused. How did these guys manage to be absent for so long and hope to pass the class?

Christmas was uneventful and a regular workday with dinner and diarrhea courtesy of the TGIF Saudi chain. New Year's was a different kettle of fish, bordering on debauchery—at least for Saudi, it was. We were invited to an embassy party, and due to the nature of the celebration, cell phones and any photographic devices were removed from the guests before entry. While the specific embassy will not be named, this was the first and last time we went to an embassy party.

The embassy party life, even more so than compound parties, was expensive, pretentious and a nightmare to get to and from. In order to be invited to an embassy party, you needed to pay a membership fee, which gave you the ability to buy tickets (pricey) for parties for you and a few friends. The membership fee was over $600, while the party tickets where between $30 and $100, depending on the party.

We were fortunate to have met a Spanish engineer, named Pablo, who had connections to most embassy parties. Fortnightly, foreigners would get together and travel to the desert to do hikes. Some were fun; some were uneventful. It didn't really matter to us either way, since we used any excuse to get outside for exercise.

The final desert walk proved to be the best. We walked through an ancient canyon, flanked by a perennial river. The river bed was dry, and I managed to find plenty of fossils, such as ammonites, trilobites and petrified wood.

We bumped into Pablo while surveying the river bed, and he was quite knowledgeable about the rock strata and age approximations. After that, we became fast friends, and it was thanks to him that we stood at the entrance of a New Year's Eve party at an embassy.

This was definitely not something that most were privy to. The embassy district was located in a restricted part of the city. After a spate of bombings in the mid 2000's, security was increased, and access to the area was boom gate controlled.

Our driver got increasingly nervous as we approached the restricted access area. Once Liz and I showed our passports, we were waved on by the security guard. Our driver dropped us off, and noticing his unease, I told him that we would find our own way home. Relieved, he drove off.

After we handed over our electronic devices

and walked through metals detectors, Liz and I walked up to a raised patio, complete with a dance floor, bar, pool and (shockingly enough) a pig on a spit, complete with an apple in its mouth!

Most people were dressed up in the latest fashion wear, and many women had the side of their head shaved, with long hair on the top and other side. Apparently this hairstyle was all the rave in Europe.

It wasn't long before the music started blaring and sweaty, scantily-dressed bodies found their way to dance floor. There was no moonshine or bathtub alcohol on sale, but there was real beer and whiskey! I drank an Amstel and wondered why I had enjoyed it before. The beer wasn't bad, it was just that I had not had a beer in a while, so it tasted like I was drinking wet bread.

After getting a healthy helping of pig and some of the salads that were offered, Liz and I retreated to the pool area. We took off our shoes and put our feet in the water while we ate. This was pure heaven: eating a forbidden meal (they tend to taste the best), feet in a pool and the sound of the leaves in the gentle breeze. It was the closest we had come to feeling content with the world since we arrived in Saudi, and we treasured the moment.

Looking around at all the drunken people and the thought of paying exorbitant fees to experience this, we both agreed not to come back. We didn't come to Saudi to spend our hard-earned money on partying. I decided then and there to move ahead with my plan to make our own wine, which would save money.

We still felt the need to get out of the house and decided to join a triathlete club (foreigners only!). Most of the members were beginners, so the atmosphere was relaxed and fun. An event was held once every two to three weeks at a different compound to ensure our safety, while also wearing athletic gear and running through the streets. We forewent the cycling part and concentrated on swimming and running. Liz was one of the strongest swimmers in the group and would often finish well before everyone. The running aspect was a different story.

Running was such a low point for Liz that she would often finish last. After a few events, I decided to run with her and give some moral support. After the race, we all convened in a hall or mess room and had a bountiful feast, which included bacon! This was a great release from all the pent-up frustrations experienced during the week.

Soon, the weekend would be over and the workweek would start again. The new week started off with a bang. Our shuttle bus to college got a new driver, and he was a tad bit too fastidious at his job. While other shuttle drivers left the campus as soon as everyone boarded their respective buses, our driver waited a set time of 15 minutes. This may not sound like much, but everyone was generally on the bus and ready to leave two minutes after he had arrived. Nobody wanted to be at the campus any longer than they needed to.

After a few days of this, tempers began to fray, and like a repressed memory, it exploded to the surface when least expected by the most unlikely person. Jude was a mild-mannered guy, who came in, did his job and went home. He did not stand in circles and discuss the latest gossip, but he stayed in his office and worked quietly.

This all changed the fifth day of our 15-minute wait. I was on my computer, watching Battlestar Galactica, of course, when I heard heavy breathing next to me over the high volume of my earphones. I looked to my side and besides the heavy breathing, Jude's face was crimson red. He got up and stormed to the front of bus to confront the driver, who, incidentally, could not even speak a word of English.

"Listen here, sonny boy!" Jude shouted. "Get this damn bus moving or else I will shove my fist down your throat. You hear me? I'm not mucking around with you!"

The driver looked confused, raising his hands to show that he did not understand. Someone from the back of the bus told a fuming Jude to leave the driver alone, because he did not speak English and was only doing his job. After a few seconds of looking around the rest of the faces on the bus, Jude came to his senses and walked dejectedly back to his seat. For the rest of the term, we always got home 15 minutes later than we needed to. Thankfully, Jude did not find himself on a one-way ticket back home.

Coming home 15 minutes late one afternoon, Liz and I decide that we wanted to be as far away from our apartment as possible, and we worked on a schedule to keep us busy for the weekend. First stop, the museum, then IKEA and, finally, the zoo.

The museum was surprisingly well-stocked. As we entered the museum, we were greeted with a mammoth and a mastodon. Flanked on the wall was a plethora of fossils, dating back from the time of the dinosaur to the dawn of mankind. A copy of the Rosetta Stone was a nice touch, along with pottery, utensils and weapons made by the earliest inhabitants of the area.

There was a mural on a wall discussing how the Earth was formed 4.7 billion years ago, which I found interesting. Since the church and state worked together as one body, I came to the tentative conclusion that Islam did not subscribe to Creationism. This was later confirmed by Sath. He said that Islam did not dispute the creation of the Earth according to science, it merely stated that science was discovering how Allah made it.

The last leg of the museum was dedicated to King Abdul-Aziz, who overthrew another ruling faction and created the modern Arabia, even lending his name, Saudi, to it. Items of interest included his pistol and breach-loaded rifle, typewriter, thobe and sword. The Arabian sword, more so than the guns, was held in high esteem, so much so that it even appeared on the flag.

The very last display was a collection of the king's cars, dating back to the 1920's, 30's, 40's and 50's.

IKEA wasn't exactly around the corner, but the drive allowed us to see new places in the city. We drove past the Intercontinental Hotel, and to my amazement, in the middle of the city was a walled off golf course. I made a mental note to return to play a round of golf sometime.

Eventually, we arrived at the large blue and yellow building, ready to have a great lunch and find some accessories for our apartment. I had the Swedish meatballs with lingonberry jam and mashed potatoes. Liz had the salmon, which was moist and delectable. Having gone to IKEA in a few different countries, one thing that could be said was that the cafeteria was always consistent.

With satisfied bellies, we found a shopping cart and slowly window shopped along the snaking trail, waiting for something to catch our eye. We didn't have to wait long for our first keeper. We suffered with a lack of cutting space in our kitchen and happened upon a dual cart and cutting station. Fruit and vegetables could be stored at the bottom, while our knife block sat perfectly at the top.

Knowing that we didn't have the largest apartment in the world, we kept our purchases to only practical necessities. Moving through the different rooms built up quite an appetite and before leaving IKEA, we had a few hot dogs and soda, ready for our next leg of our journey.

The saddest place in the whole world, we decided, was the Riyadh Zoo. That was our first and final impression of it. It didn't help that it was over a hundred and ten degrees at 5pm in the afternoon. The animals looked listless and tired with glazed eyes. Crowds of people surrounded the lion's enclosure, heckling it and throwing objects at it to try to elicit a reaction. They were sorely mistaken, and the lion laid in a half dead stupor. I'm sure if it had the ability to commit suicide, it would have a long time ago.

Looking around at the calamity going on at various animal pens, we quickly realized that we did not want to be there long and walked out the front gate, just 10 minutes after having arrived at the zoo.

We remembered seeing a Mexican restaurant close to the zoo and decided to walk over. One thing that always amazed me with walking downtown was that, while the roads were congested, the sidewalks were all but empty. It had just about confirmed that Saudi did not have a walking culture.

We were surprised to meet some of Liz's colleagues at the restaurant, and we decided to make one, big table. The food was great, and for just that moment, we let down our guard and had a relaxed dinner party.

At times, I forgot that we were in Saudi, and this proved to be a great escape from the inequities that bound us in the country of Allah's chosen people, the magical Kingdom of Saudi Arabia. The only thing that was missing was my wine, but there was more to life than alcohol. Eventually, we made it home by 9pm, ready for a new week of "work".

A few days later, I came home with midnight run gossip and ran into the room, only to find Liz laying on the bed with tears in her eyes. Rushing over to her, she raised her hand to indicate that she was fine and just needed a moment. I gave her space and started dinner.

Standing at the entrance of the kitchen, Liz asked, "Do you remember that movie you made me watch before coming to Saudi?"

"*Not without My Daughter*, yes?" I replied.

"Yes. Even though you found it funny to show it to me, it did affect me. It made me sad to think that if a woman is divorced in Islam, she has no say over her children and they are obliged to stay with the father.

I haven't thought about the movie for the longest time until today. A colleague of mine, Mary, broke down in tears today and needed someone to talk to, so we found an empty classroom. She is originally from Wales and met an old, rich Saudi when she was in her late teens. He swept her off her feet and showered her with gifts. They got married and lived in Wales for five years and had two kids. Missing home, her husband convinced her to move the family to Saudi. That was the day her life changed drastically.

"Once in Saudi, her husband changed and became cold and distant. Later, she found out that her husband, who was now well into his sixties, was planning on marrying a seventeen-year-old girl. She was horrified and wanted to go back home. When she voiced her concerns to her husband, he divorced her in the Islamic traditional way of simply saying "talak" three times. That was it, no judges and courts—just three words.

"She was allowed to leave, but she discovered that according to Saudi law, she had no say in the lives and wellbeing of her children. They had to stay in Saudi with their father. Distraught, she went back to Wales for a few months, but realizing that she could not spend another day without seeing her children, she found a teaching job in Saudi and saw her kids most weekends.

"Everything seemed to be okay, for the most part, until the new wife discovered she was pregnant. The new wife became territorial and catty, often telling Mary that she was not welcome there anymore, in not so many words. It all came to a head last week when, at the insistence of the new wife, Mary's ex-husband asked her not to come around anymore... even to see the children.

"It just breaks my heart to see her in so much pain. The worst part is that she has no solution to the problem and seems resigned to just go home a broken person."

A week after Liz told me this story, she found out that Mary had left Saudi, and unlike a Hollywood movie, there was no happy ending.

CHAPTER 5
The Beginning of the End

As the days turned into weeks, the weather started to make a steady increase from hot to inferno. It was at this time that we started going downtown and trying out many different restaurants to mix into our daily diet of Middle Eastern food.

The first restaurant we tried was Korean. Getting there proved to be a bit difficult. Our taxi driver seemed like he was drugged or high on life, randomly singing, swerving around invisible barriers and constantly reminding us where he was from. My fault, I guess. I enjoy speaking to people from other countries and usually ask where they are from, the popular food of the area and so forth. Like most people that are proud of their country and language, he insisted I get the pronunciation right.

"Sooo ooww diiiii…"

"You are from Saudi Arabia?"

"Laa, Laa, Soooo oow diii…"

We went back and forth until he was happy

with my pronunciation. To my ear, all ten attempts sounded exactly the same.

Finally, we arrived at the address displayed on the restaurant's website, but the place was empty and abandoned. The area was a construction zone. The entrance of the worksite had a big poster proclaiming it to be the future site of a library named after the current king.

We walked the site that probably should have been cordoned off because of all the heavy equipment, tools and partially finished structures, and we found our way back to the city center on the other side of the building.

While walking through the work site, we had noticed that it was the future home of a library, dedicated to the king. After asking other business owners in the area, we were eventually told that the Korean restaurant had moved over a couple blocks on the other side of the city. We decided to walk to the restaurant and used the walk as a way of familiarizing ourselves with the city.

We passed two of the largest buildings on our way: first, the Faisaliah Tower and, next, the Kingdom Tower. It was about a mile and a half between the towers, and since Saudi is not a pedestrian friendly or even a pedestrian culture, we found ourselves alone in the back alleys.

It was a cathartic experience in the cool of the evening, and in the months following, we would often return to do the walk between the towers, as it felt freeing to spend some time out in the open.

We would also alternate between the two towers, shopping in their respective malls and doing further walks around them.

On this particular night, we eventually reached the Korean restaurant, and after that unexpected workout, I was ready to be fed. The food was nostalgic of our time spent in Korea, and it was the most authentic we had since leaving Korea.

Liz had the Kimchi Jigae, and I had Bulgogi Galbi. The bountiful banchan of many different flavors rounded off the gastronomic experience. It was not cheap, but we had found our home away from home. When our waiter arrived to clear our table, I joking told him that we would take two beers. He laughed nervously and shuffled away quickly. I wondered if I hit a nerve but quickly forgot about it. A few minutes later he came out with our desserts and looked me in the eye and said, "Please don't drink alcohol in Saudi, please."

I looked at him perplexed and saw that he had the tears in his eyes.

"I was at a party not too far away from here and the *Mutaween* were called. I was arrested, my hands were tied to a pole and I was whipped countless times. I don't want this to happen to anyone else, please be careful. You and your wife."

The reality of our situation of being in a country with a poor human rights records hit us like a sledgehammer.

While thanking the waiter for his warning and apologizing for what happened, the owner came past our table. After a few pleasantries were exchanged, we discovered that he was from Korea but left after the fall of the military-style government in the 1980s. He had made Saudi his self-imposed exile country of choice, and he vowed only to return to Korea once the people had come to the realization that only the army was fit to run the country, especially since it had officially been at war for the past 50 years.

Whatever his stance was regarding Korea, one thing that could be said was that he was passionate about his country and expressed this in the way he prepared our authentic feast. In parting, he thanked us for what he saw as us doing a service to his country having taught there, and he advised us to come back on Saturday evening for the buffet. He did not have to ask us twice.

Proceeding into the first month of classes, the old habits of my students slowly reared their ugly heads. It was difficult to communicate with them, since their English was so poor. However, one thing I did gather from some of my students, when pressed, was that they were not interested in the class and just joined the university for money.

I was also asked to accept Mohamed as my prophet, since that was the only way to be led to a profitable life. I told them I would consider it, and the next day, while waiting at the entrance of my classroom, a few of my students brought in pots of delicious smelling food and greeted me in the traditional Saudi manner of rubbing our noses and kissing both cheeks. I was first taken aback and then confused. In total, I had 14 students, and we pushed the chairs back and sat on a mat in the front of the classroom.

The student with the best English told me that the class wanted to show me what Saudi cuisine really was like. It then hit me like a ton of bricks, and I was very touched at their thoughtfulness. The previous day, in passing, I had mentioned to my students that most of the food I thought was Saudi was actually from other Middle Eastern countries, and I wasn't sure what authentic Saudi food was. The students felt that it was their obligation to show me a taste of traditional Saudi cuisine.

The meal was strange. The students called it old man's ears as the homemade pasta was thick and shaped like ears. The rest of the dish was ground beef with a white sauce. It was not fine dining by any stretch of the imagination, but it was hearty food that stuck to your gut. Food for the people. The students were also generous to provide a small pot of the same food to take home for my wife.

Instead of class the next day, one of the students, Ibrahim, invited the class to his family's camel farm. I readily agreed and thought it would be a great way of practicing the English of objects and scenes in the students' everyday life.

Liz had settled into a routine with her female students and would often regale the office intrigue over dinner. While she ate the "old man's ears" her stories were definitely more interesting than normal days.

"Well, Doran made us wait again! Every morning we have to wait for her. This morning, she strolled to the shuttle and complained that she had to rush eating her pomegranate. Upon hearing this someone at the back who had heard quite enough said, 'How dare the driver come on time! What is this world coming to?' There was muffled laughter, but I doubt this will change Doran's habits anytime soon. It seemed like the joke, just like her tardiness, went over her head. Takes all kinds, I guess.

"Anyway, when we got to school, everyone was talking about a prayer meeting between some of the foreign Muslim staff. There is this inner circle of foreign Muslims on campus that include the assistant dean, Tranquility. She is African American, which is integral to understanding the animosity that occurred. The other members of the inner circle included some supervisors and teachers.

"Anyway, one of the teachers, who formed part of the inner circle, was angry with Tranquility because she went off on a tangent during one of the prayer meetings. Yasmine, the teacher from South Africa who is part of the inner circle, was highly offended when Tranquility started using a South

African racial slur. I'm not sure what the word was, but it translated from Hebrew to a word meaning 'unbeliever'. Tranquility was using the word to describe the non-Muslim teachers at the college."

I interrupted Liz's story to add some of my own thoughts on the matter: "Phelani Thabo, one of my colleagues from South Africa, gave me a brief history of the country, and he mentioned that the white, racist minority, during Apartheid, would call black South Africans by this name."

According to Phelani, Apartheid was a period between 1652 to 1994, where a white minority stole the lands from the local inhabitants and took all the country's vast mineral wealth, while leaving the native people to live in squalor. Of all the gold mined throughout history, 30% of it was mined in South Africa in the last 150 years. Unlike Saudi, which shares its oil wealth with its citizen, South Africa's wealth is horded by an elite minority.

"Anyways," I continued, "the word begins with a 'k', but I'm not going to utter it as it has a strong history of dehumanizing an entire group of people. Phelani mentioned that unlike the African Americans who keep the 'n' word in their vocabulary as a way of taking back the word, South African blacks acknowledged that they can never take back a word that was never theirs to begin with, and in the same breath, they would never want that word to be uttered again. Most are hoping that it gets buried alongside Apartheid. It is a powerful word that Phelani refused to mention.

"So, I can understand the reaction from the South African teacher. Phelani went on to mention that the Apartheid Reformist Government in South Africa helped Israel create an atomic bomb in the 70's, since they felt it was their duty to help the first believers. The 'k' word was believed to be a derivative of Hebrew meaning rock/slave/unbeliever, depending on whom you ask."

"Wow," Liz cut back in. "When you start to talk, you just don't know when to stop. Anyway, moving on with the story, the South African teacher was angry and confronted Tranquility for using the word and stormed out of the prayer meeting. She told the other South African teachers and there were a few angry teachers wanting to talk to Tranquility. Regardless if they were Muslim or not, it was not acceptable to use that word. Conveniently, Tranquility took the rest of the week off. By next week, this will have blown over, and there would be a new story.

"Well, I didn't need to wait that long for my next fix. Agnes, who is British Nigerian, asked me to help her with file merging her class records. I started by making a new file as a template and putting it in her documents folder. Low and behold, her documents' folder was full of pornography. Pictures, videos, you name it. She is close to sixty and a highly devoted Muslim. I really didn't see that one coming. So, I pretended I didn't see it, did what I needed to do and got out of her office.

"If anyone else saw those files while I was working on her computer, I would have been thrown in prison. I will use this as an example and never offer my services again to anyone.

"Just when I figured it couldn't get any worse, when I got to class, my partner teacher was missing. At our campus, we have a class for two hours and then swap students with another teacher and take theirs. This tandem teaching helps to relieve some of the pressure of seeing the same students for four hours a day.

"Anyways, she was gone, just like that. A midnight runner. The interesting thing about her was that she was single and pregnant. This could carry a long prison sentence for her if found out, so she wore a long, loose-fitting, black dress every day. A few teachers had made a few comments that she was starting to put on weight, but no one ever caught on for six months. She was hopeful to get a few more paychecks, but just like that, she left.

"Until they find a replacement, I am stuck with my students for four hours a day. I'm not sure how long finding another partner teacher is going to take." Liz sighed, before ending her story. "I guess what I've learned is that there really is a shortage of women teachers at the college."

The next day, one of my students, Abdul-Aziz, picked me up at the university. The city of Riyadh is set up so that there is one main highway that starts at the city center, and after every mile or two there is an exit that leads to a suburb. We lived off of exit 8, called Ishbilia.

When Abdul-Aziz and I arrived at the main road, instead of driving left towards the city center, we turned right into the unknown. This was my first time going in this direction, and I was interested to see what lay ahead.

While I kept the conversation light, asking about his family, favorite food, movie, etc., my eyes wandered over the landscape that quickly turned from low-rise apartments and homes to scattered settlements and then to stark, beige, rock outcrops, sand and dust.

"While I kept my eyes focused on the land, Abdul-Aziz began to talk about how his grandfather still lived a strict Bedouin lifestyle in the desert. One day, his grandfather had come to their home and, upon seeing a television in the home, fell into a fit of rage and systematically destroyed every T.V. in the house.

The thing that bothered Abdul-Aziz the most about this episode was that he could not play videogames anymore. At the time, single young men were banned from going to malls. Thus, there was not much else in terms of entertainment. So, videogames was his escape, and now that had been taken away by his grandfather.

Liz and I found out about the mall ban the hard way. During a company shopping trip, the men were dropped off at a different entrance from the ladies. Liz went into the mall, and the other males and I were stopped and threatened with incarceration. After about a half an hour of shopping, Liz became quite concerned as to where I was. Needless to say, we bought cell phones that very day.

We went off the highway and onto a dirt road. After 5 miles of driving through the desert, we were hit with a strong, animal feedlot aroma. I found it interesting that the land was mainly comprised of rocky outcrops instead of just sand and more sand.

Abdul-Aziz told me that the center of the country was rocky with canyons and mountains. However, in the south, the Rub' al Khali desert, also known as "The Empty Quarter", was mainly just sand. He mentioned that the male members of his family raced their dune buggies in that area.

"What about the ladies in your family?" I asked.

Abdul-Aziz mentioned that ladies were not allowed to drive, so they stayed at home.

We took a turn off the dirt road and happened upon a sea of camels. The farm was nestled between two ridges, and the image was picture perfect for a post card. I told Abdul-Aziz that I was upset that I did not bring my camera with, so he offered to take some pictures of us with his phone and send me a picture of our trip together later. (I never did get the pictures.)

Ibrahim greeted us in the traditional Saudi way of rubbing our noses together. As I was unaccustomed to this, it felt weird, but not wanting to offend, I took it in stride. Ibrahim directed us to a Bedouin tent overlooking the camel enclosure. It was adorned with beautiful Persian tapestries, and the floor had mosaic designed carpets that were made of silk and were soft to the touch.

It was, in fact, the best carpet I had ever felt, and I had to ask where the family bought it. It turned out that the carpet had been in their family for 3 generations and where and how much it cost was lost to memory. In the center of the carpet was a hookah, and we all sat around it, taking turns smoking the cherry-flavored tobacco.

The conversation was light, comprising of the who's, what's, why's and how's that pertain to general topics, such as food, movies, video games and so forth. One of the students asked if I was a Muslim, and when I looked up to answer, I noticed that all the students were looking at me. I shook my head, but I added that we all still believed in the same God. One nodded his head but pointed up to the sky, and with a look of sheer ecstasy, said that Allah is God and Mohamed is his prophet. I smiled, nodded and, not wanting to discuss this further, I asked my students if they wanted more than one wife.

Sath had told me that allowing men to marry up to four women in Islam was in response to the disproportionate number of females to males. He suspected that it had very little to do with the natural birth rate but much to do with the wars fought in the name is Islam over the first couple centuries of the religion. Sath mentioned that the current birth rate of 52 females to 48 males was in line with global averages.

As soon as I asked the question, Abdul-Aziz shook his head almost violently. He went on to say that from personal experience (his father had 3 wives), he did not think it was a good idea. In order to have more than one wife, you have to give them the same standard of living. This means that you have to provide equally to each family, which was becoming harder and harder to accomplish in the current economy. Each family needed its own house, because wives do not live together.

When his family were Bedouin, a generation ago, life was cheap. All a man needed was his animals and a good tent, and he could have 4 wives with ease. The price of homes, clothing, food, etc. in the cities were now expensive. He said that he would rather have one wife and be able to afford all that he needs without the daily stress of trying to make it work. Finally, he said that even the lack of money was not as bad as the constant drama of having to take care of 3 households. It meant that one had to constantly bounce from house to house, trying to solve problems. Family trips, even to the desert, were a logistic nightmare, and in the last five years, his father had become an absent parent, often choosing to simply spend time with friends or in his room.

Abdul-Aziz said that he did not want that life. Having more than one wife was something of a fantasy for most men, but as the old adage goes, "Be careful what you wish for, you may just get it."

Back at the men's lunch and a few more trivial conversations, Ibrahim gave us a tour of his family's camel farm on a dune buggy. We zipped past camels that made the most interesting sounds, reminiscent of a wailing banshee. One of his brothers was in the process of milking a female camel, which was interestingly called a cow.

We all got out of the buggy, and Ibrahim's brother called us over. He passed around the glazed, clay pot filled with camel's milk, and each of us took a drink. The milk had a rich and creamy taste, with a slight saltiness at the back of the palate.

After I drank, a couple of the students started to laugh. Confused, I smiled and asked what was funny, and they pointed at the milk. My mind started racing. Had the students done something unspeakable to the milk?

Laughing as well, Ibrahim pointed to the milk and said that if this was my first time drinking camel's milk that I was in for a surprise and that I would get a powerful bowel movement later. The rest of the day, the thought of getting violent diarrhea was at the top of my mind. Thankfully, it didn't ever actually come.

"You did what! Are you crazy?" Sam, an Australian teacher who worked in many cities in Saudi, was dumbfounded when I mentioned that I went with my students into the desert.

"When I worked at Hofuf, a small town on the east coast, something terrible happened. It is because of that I will never go to isolated places with Saudi students."

Since this was our campus lunch break, teachers involved in private discussions stopped and turned towards Sam. It's as if everyone needed his daily cup of scandal.

He looked around and then began his story. "My colleague Rodney was invited to the desert with his students, and when they arrived at an unmarked location, the students held him down and took turns raping him. They said they had to teach him a lesson for speaking ill of the Prophet Mohamed.

"Thankfully, he wasn't killed but when he went to the head teacher to report the crime, he was told that if he ever mentions this to anyone, it could mean the death sentence for him. Homosexual acts both wanted and unwanted are illegal in Saudi. Being a foreigner and making accusations against a Saudi was a serious business, and regardless of the injustices, you are bound to lose. He decided to leave Saudi, and I have not heard from him again."

Everyone's faces ranged from being flabbergasted to shell-shocked. After a long pause, Sam ended with, "And that is why I will never go out with my students alone."

"Bullshit!" exclaimed Tristan, who, at the age of

28, was a Saudi veteran of the past 3 years. His big plan was to save money and invest in the stock market. "I have heard many questionable Saudi stories, but this one takes the cake."

"I was there, and it happened," Sam replied nonchalantly.

"I bet you were there, and that's why you can't sit anymore. "

After some muffled laughter, Sam walked away, just simply saying that it really was true and to think twice about excursions with students.

Over the course of the next couple of days, Sam remained defiant and insisted that the story was true. Some people became visibly shaken with this realization. I do not know if Sam was lying or not, but even after my positive experience at the camel farm, I never went out with my students again. In hindsight, I feel as if I let my biases get the better of me, and for that I am ashamed.

Every afternoon, I would come home and see a plastic trash can with cardboard boxes of juice at our foyer. Today was the day that I would begin the process of converting this juice into the nectar of the gods. Without getting into too many details, I followed the instructions that I meticulously took on the compound and let Mother Nature do the rest. I added my own special touches here and there, such as adding some strawberries for a pleasant note when drinking—well that was the hope anyways.

From time to time, while sitting at work, I would daydream about my apartment getting raided. This bothered me for the longest time because of the repercussions. This heightened sense of anxiety led me to a few realizations. Number one: the wine (its preparation, distribution and drinking) was on a strict need-to-know basis, and nobody except my most trusted friends needed to know. The stakes were too high.

There were many days that I considered dumping the wine-to-be down the drain, but my fortitude got the better of me. All throughout this time, I had to fight the constant urge to sample the wine, but I stayed strong and didn't open the lid. One Friday, about two weeks later, Liz and I decided to "uncork" the wine and sample the nectar of the gods (Was there a god of trash cans in the Greek Parthenon?) The strawberry notes were subtle, but unmistakable. The wine itself was semi-sweet and surprisingly pleasant. I could not believe it. First time was a charm!

The teacher apartment blocks were an interesting beast. Since the company housed over a thousand teachers from 5 different universities, teachers were housed in apartment blocks all over the city. Teachers from different countries and religious backgrounds were lumped together. Except for couples, which were offered a one-bedroom apartment, unmarried teachers had to share a two-bedroom apartment. This did much to create many issues and scandalous stories to satiate bored men and ladies while sitting around their respective groups.

We lived on the 2nd floor of an apartment, and our neighbors were as diverse as a floor could be. At the bottom of the hall on the right was a British Nigerian Muslim who practiced the Saudi style of marriage. He had one wife in England, and the other lived with him in his apartment. A British Kenyan lived next to him, and he shared his apartment with a Texan. Both were in their late fifties and Muslim.

Directly across from us lived a middle-aged South African named Ben, who bared a stunning resemblance to Ernest Hemingway, and a younger American, named Vergil. We became good friends with the latter apartment.

While single men dominated roadside restaurants, woman, unless there was a "family" section, could not eat at the restaurant. The opposite was true for malls. Single men could not eat at a sit-down restaurant unless they were married or part of a family that included a lady. Ben and Vergil had been interested in eating at the Turkish restaurant, but since they were males, they were constantly turned away. Being turned away did not stop them from trying every once in a while, but on Friday, we worked it out that we would all go. Ben was Liz's father, and Vergil was my brother, if asked. Everything went off without a hitch, and after that, we would go out together to different restaurants from time to time.

After tasting the wine, just to make sure I was not biased, I gave Ben and Vergil a bottle and hoped to hear their thoughts. The next day, around 12, there was a knock on our door. This was unusual as we rarely, if ever, entertained at home. Fearing the worst, I covered the trash can with a couch throw and put a potted plant on it. When I peered through the door's peephole, Vergil waved the empty, liter, soda bottle in his hand, while Ben knocked on the door.

I opened the door and hastily brought them in. Giggling, they said that they wanted to report back on how the wine was. Both loved the wine and had finished the bottle in 30 minutes. This was the first time that both of them had drank in months, so they both looked like cheap dates. Success! I filled their bottle and sent them on their way. Shortly after, we left for the afternoon to explore other sections of the city.

Liz and I had heard of two old sections of the city called the Masmak and Batha. Both were *souks*, which are open air markets, selling goods of all shapes and sizes. We decided to explore first Masmak, for its historic significance.

Masmak was a large, clay, mud brick- and straw-built fort with four watchtowers. It was located in the old quarter and built on an oasis. It was used as a halfway rest area, whilst traveling from the two coasts.

The fort itself had an interesting history and was the site of the battle where the Saud family wrestled control over the leadership of the country by overthrowing an Emirati usurper. He was so overjoyed with his victory, that he named the country after himself.

Once we entered the fort, it felt like we were transported to the movie set of Lawrence of Arabia. The fort was large, considering it was made of clay and mud brick.

During the tour, we were first shown an open atrium were troops could assemble. There were pens for the horses and animals, but the most striking part of the fort was the living rooms. They were not living rooms by western standards, but well-ventilated, square rooms with carpets on the floor and an open fire in the center. Since it was hot, the fireplace was not lit, but there was a pyramid of wood to show where it was purposed to be.

The guests were asked to take a seat on the floor, and employees came around serving Arabian coffee. We all formed a circle with the people closest to us and relaxed on the ornate cushions on the floor. Just for that moment, we felt what it was like to be an Arab, living circa early 1900's.

The rest of the group exchanged pleasantries, and before we knew it, we were escorted out of the room, and the tour continued. It was interesting to hear the history of the place, and I was surprised that the king, even after he became wealthy from oil, lived in the fort up until 1938.

Masmak Fort was surrounded by a *souk*, and after the tour, Liz and I decided to explore as much as we could. The first point of interest close to the fort was called Deera Square, or colloquially Chop-Chop Square. This was the place where executions were carried out. Just our luck, a crowd was gathered around the square. I pointed to the square and asked someone what was going on, and he simply placed his hand behind his neck in a chopping motion.

Liz and I looked at each other with our mouths agape, both knowing what the other one was thinking. Do we stay or go? Curiosity got the better of us, and we decided to stay. I read in a book that Saudis generally encouraged foreigners to move to the front of the crowd to see firsthand what may happen to them if they break the law. This time was no different. As we moved within the crowd, talking to a few people who could speak English, we were told to move forward with a quick pointing back-and-forth gesture.

We eventually made it to the front of the crowd. We were still a distance from the condemned man, but we were close enough to see the ritual. The sword was sharp, the act was swift.

We were horrified and backtracked out of the crowd across the road into a *souk*. I'm not sure if I had blacked out or erased the scene from my mind, but when I think back at the moment, it seems like a dreamlike haze. I wish I could take that moment back and choose not to witness the barbaric act. I feel as if watching it lent credence and my approval. We walked around the souk in a daze, and finally decided to go home, vowing never to return.

During a call to prayer, between classes, we were sitting around exchanging stories of our weekend, when Rex appeared out of nowhere. I had not seen him in months, and the rumor going around was that he got himself out of teaching and was an administrator in another wing of the college. He sat down and began to talk as if the last time we spoke was yesterday.

"The more I stay in this country, the more I realize that this country is one, big, mind-control, brainwashing experiment gone wrong," remarked Rex.

While Rex had not been around in a long-time, he was well respected, and his opinions carried weight. "In the army, we were briefed on the tenets of successful brainwashing. We studied cults and totalitarian regimes, and much of that seems to apply here. Granted, it can be argued that this is a fundamental religious autocracy, which checks off all the requirements for a brainwashing regime. They control the news and media, make sure their populous is tired and cannot think straight with the weird calls of mandatory prayer hours, both at night and early in the morning, and enforce the conformity of making everyone wear the same clothing."

Ironically enough, Sam, finding the conversation uncomfortable, changed the subject and asked what Rex was doing these days, since we had not seen him in a while.

"Degree verifications," Rex shot back. "I have already found two people who lied about their degrees and sent them home. When I was in Thailand, there was a street that specialized in being the center of fake degrees. I know guys who 'got' their doctorate in a few hours. This is harmful for the students and for the university. If I had my way, I would charge the teachers for fraud. Doesn't really matter in the end. Most of the teachers that come to Saudi from Thailand leave within the first month. They literally came from paradise on Earth to hell on Earth. Stats never lie! Anyway, back to the grindstone... keep your chins up, lads!"

And just like that, Typhoon Rex swept by, leaving a few people with an extra dose of anxiety in his wake.

Sitting around and hearing a new, true-life, horror story everyday was beginning to take its toll on some. A new recruit, Dane, discovered that there was a gym close by, and the more people who signed up together, the cheaper the discount. It didn't take much to convince me and straight after lunch, we took a walk over to the gym. Dane was our point man and started chatting with the sales consultant. I stared off in the distance, watching the French Open tennis tournament until I was shaken out of my dreamlike state with Dane pointing to the salesman saying, "Listen here, Ali Baba, we had a deal. I brought the people for the discount and now you are changing the rules. Listen here, Ali Baba. That's not how we do things in Baltimore."

All the while, Dane was pointing and shouting at the salesman, the salesman's eyes were getting bigger and bigger, until they were as large as saucers.

The salesman yelled back, "Who Ali Baba? Who Ali Baba!?"

I slowly backed my way out of the gym, during the commotion, hoping that I would not be remembered when I decided to come back a few days later. I needed the gym, and I was determined to give it a day or two.

Impatiently, the next day, I went back to the gym. Thankfully, there was a different person at the front desk. I quickly applied for my membership, and in 10 minutes, I was sitting in the sauna, sweating away my iniquities.

Walking back to the university, Duncan was in the street having a heated argument with his roommate. A crowd of people were pointing and starting to gather. Knowing that if the police showed up, both would be put in prison, I called out to Duncan, pointing to all the people who were gathering. He snapped out of his anger and walked towards me. I knew of a quiet Syrian restaurant close by, and we decided to make our way there as quickly as possible.

"I'm going to wring his neck!" Duncan exclaimed.

"Easy does it...." I said. "What happened?"

"I have this new roommate, Smithe, a Brit. There has been a spat of people miraculously converting to Islam in order to gain *wasta*, which is Arabic for favor, hoping for better treatment and job promotions. He did the conversion bit a few weeks ago and is now taking it to his head. He wants me to put off the T.V. during the call to prayer, does not want friends of both sexes in the apartment and so on. He has also been running back and carrying tales to the administration. I just got called into a meeting to explain why I was being disrespectful of Islam. The worst part is that he does not have any interest in the religion and is obviously using it to further his own agenda. The administration is eating it up because they are proud that a young, white, British male has seen the 'error in his ways' and now submits to the will of Allah."

Venting seemed to help Duncan's rage a bit. Having managed to calm down and come up with a plan, we departed the restaurant for our afternoon classes. Duncan, along with a few disgruntled employees, going through their own issues, banded together and decided to take their housing stipend to rent a villa and a van for transport.

I was wondering if this day could get any more interesting, and it did not fail to oblige...

On the shuttle drive home, which was generally a quiet affair of people lost on their phones, computers, media players or simply staring vacantly out the window, the atmosphere became highly charged.

Boko Haram, a Nigerian Islamic terrorist group, or freedom fighters, depending on who you asked, was being discussed by two teachers. They were highlighting the brutality of the group, attacking schools and taking the girls as wives, because they believed that woman should never be educated. My Kenyan-British neighbor, Karim, heard the conversation and pointed out that Boko Haram stood for Islamic principles and did not want western ideals permeating their society. He indicated that they fight the depravity of the west and that he stands by them.

Totally gob smacked, the two teachers, not knowing how to respond, retreated back into a daze, staring at their phones. We had learned that speaking out about atrocities committed by any Muslim was a faux pas, regardless of whether they were right or wrong.

A few weeks before, we had just got a new shuttle driver. He was always late, and a few of the teachers began to get disgruntled. One teacher, Rob, asked the driver if he would be on time tomorrow. The driver replied with the word "*inshallah*", which means "if God wills it". This was a commonly used term by Muslims when asked if something would be done. It was believed that all things were done if God willed them, and if something else came up, it was His will as well. This sentiment became a running joke as whenever one heard the fateful word "*inshallah*", they knew they didn't have a dog's chance of getting things done.

The Islamic version of the Abrahamic God was an interesting character. He tirelessly worked behind the scenes to take care of every facet of the believers' lives, yet the mindsets of the believers were the complete converse, sitting back and waiting for things to happen and calling it "His" will if it didn't.

Unsurprisingly, the driver was late the next day, and when asked if he would come on time tomorrow, he nodded his head again and said, "*Inshallah*."

Another teacher at the back asked Rob what the driver said and he retorted, "The driver said '*inshallah*', which as you know, means 'go fuck yourself'."

There were gasps, and all the Muslims teachers on the bus stared at Rob.

The colleague sitting next to me pointed outside to a pile of dirt on the horizon. "Did you know that even though Saudi is basically a big sand pit, even the dirt has to be imported? It is believed that the desert sand is too round from erosion, so it does not bind well to the mortar..."

"Interesting," I commented, staring out the window and hoping to be somewhere else.

The very next day, Rob was called out of class,

driven to his apartment to pack and was sent home.

People knew where they stood after this.

We had no doubt that it was Karim. He had become bitter over the last couple of months. While Islam had preached equality, he had often found himself on the receiving end of racism. Police would stop him and ask for his passport on the street and while standing in lines others who were not black were called to the front of the line ahead of him.

The *coup de grace* came when a white, British colleague told him that since Saudi has a Barclay's bank branch, he could send his money home cheaper and easier. When Karim went to the bank with all his documents in hand, they took one look at him and sent him away.

Coming home to a glass of wine and a hot bath was akin to Heaven. The magical kingdom was starting to get to me. I felt as if I needed to put my head down and just be anonymous for the next week. I repeated the mantra, "Focus on making money."

We needed a change of scenery, because school was becoming toxic for both of us. Duncan told me and a few other people in confidence about a new compound called Al Raji, which was close to us and that had a wonderful restaurant. We were told to text our names and nationalities to the head waiter, and he would put our name on a list held by the front gate security.

It worked. The next night, we breezed through security and found ourselves at a quaint, bistro-style restaurant with French and English items on the menu. I had a slow roasted lamb shank basted with a tikka sauce and Liz had white fish with a white wine reduction, garlic mash and oven roasted parmesan asparagus. The food was delectable, and we were surprised to find out that the restaurant sold its own wine, made in-house. We were reluctant to try it at first, but after sharing a glass of wine, we realized that it was good, but not as good as mine. However, it was on par with the other compound, and we were pleased.

We were able to spend one more evening there, having dinner, singing karaoke and listening to Meatloaf's "Bat out of Hell", before an anonymous call was made to the religious police. They warned the compound that it would be closed if they continued to sell alcohol.

Through the grapevine, we heard two stories that contributed to the place not accepting non-compound residents for dinner and drinks anymore. Duncan mentioned that one of the greenhorn teachers caught wind of the compound and spoke loudly about it on the shuttle home. He suspected that one of the Muslim teachers heard this and sent an anonymous tip to the religious police. The irony of this was that the guy, who was suspected of calling the religious police, left within the month.

The story to his sudden departure is as follows, he was a handsome guy, and after mosque one evening, a Saudi invited him to his home. Upon arriving at the house, the Saudi locked the door and stripped his clothes off. The teacher had to jump out a second-story window in order to evade his admirer.

The other story was somewhat connected to me, while being twice removed at the same time. In Korea, there were three types of teachers: public, private academy, or university. Anyone with a bachelor's degree could teach at any three school types, since they were essentially the same curriculum. The twenty-one-year-old university teachers were the funniest lot of them all. They would walk around with puffed out chests, wanting everyone to call them professor. It was nearly as funny as it was sad to see.

In our small town in Korea, my fellow public-school teachers would get together for drinks every Wednesday, and before long, two university teachers began joining us. Randy and Doug were in their late thirties, but their personalities were polar opposites in every other way. Randy was from Canada, did not drink alcohol and was very respectful towards everyone. Doug was from New York and very loud. (On occasion, he would stand on the table and scream that he was Italian. Someone would snicker, "From Florence, Kansas?" Thankfully, this did not last long.) Sadly, he was also a drunk. Doug would go on weekday benders and his school administrators would scrape him off the pavement come morning. Doug lasted a few short months, and I thought that was the last I would see of him.

After months of not having an office, a desk opened up and was offered to me. It was not an office in the traditional sense; up to sixteen guys shared a room the size of classroom. I walked into my new "office", and lo and behold, Doug was there sitting at a desk.

He looked good, well, in the sense that he looked sober, healthy and had the complete opposite personality, more akin to that of Randy's. The ESL world had many stories of burnt-out teachers using overseas teaching jobs as a way to fund their substance abuse problems, while keeping their anonymity. There was also a group of teachers who had alcohol and substance abuse problems that would come to Saudi to "dry out". The ESL world was also small, and you would often hear of teachers who met in other countries, reuniting in Saudi.

At first, Doug did not recognize me, whether it was purposeful or not, but soon we started to chat and catch up. He was engaged to a Korean lady and was working in Saudi to pay for a new home. The salaries in Saudi were, on average, a thousand dollars more a paycheck than in Korea, so it made sense. Liz and I would have gone back to Korea if their salaries were on par. However, Korea was flooded with applicants, so salaries had stagnated. Saudi, on the other hand, had a shortage of teachers. With the demand of teachers going up, so did the salaries, and that was the main reason why we were in Saudi.

Doug stuck mainly to himself and the office, which was one of the reasons I had not seen him before. It turned out that Doug got wind of Al Raji compound and went there a few times to get wasted. Apparently, he got more belligerent as time went by, and during his third outing, he refused to leave after the last call and punched the owner, breaking his nose.

"So, you know what the most offensive name in Islam is? No? Anybody? Well, its Christian Bacon," joked Duncan.

"It seems like you have an extra set of wings, since you dumped your roommate," someone shot back. "Keep plugging away, and your next roommate will be an ISIS devotee."

Duncan replied quickly, "I already have new roommate, thank you very much, and he is cool. His family is originally from Sudan, and they have been in the UK for over thirty years. We have similar music choices and support the same footy team: Manchester United, the best team in the world. He is a Muslim, but he is laid back and does not let this place get to his head. It appears that Muslims, like Christians, can have the Jerusalem Syndrome. We can call it the Mecca Syndrome."

Duncan's roommate, out of no where, also did

the midnight run a few weeks later, and after a few days of teasing Duncan that it was his smelly underwear that drove the guy to leave the country, his roommate's absence was forgotten for a while.

Two months later, our lead teacher, who was a moderate Muslim, began weeping during a meeting one day. He shared with the group a newspaper clipping of Duncan's old roommate, holding an AK 47. The headline announced his death, which occurred while fighting for the extremist group, Al-Nessra.

Duncan looked absolutely shocked and dumbfounded with the news and could not believe that his ex-roommate had that in him.

"I guess he believed he was doing the right thing," was all Duncan said, before leaving the meeting with his eyes staring at the floor.

For most people sitting in the room, the news had hit the last wind out of their sails, and now there was a legitimate fear that anyone of our colleagues could be present or future terrorists. No one ever made a joke at school about the country, religion or any aspects of the culture again. Our silence was bought with the heaviest of prices: death.

An elderly couple, Brian and Sage, had recently left Qatar due to age restrictions with employment and rented a huge villa. Liz had befriended Sage and was invited to a weekly play reading.

Brian and Sage were excellent hosts, who made scrumptious meals and delectable homemade wine. All those factors made for funny play readings, whereby every person had to read a line. The group of people coming to the play reading were interesting, and we made many new friends.

The first play was an Oscar Wilde classic entitled The Importance of Being Earnest. Different people quickly got into character, and there even was a plethora of accents being thrown around.

Liz felt bland by comparison, but I didn't let that get to me and just had a great time. I hoped to have many more of these evenings and looked forward to the next time.

Saudi was beginning to take its toll on Liz. Unlike the men, the women could not leave their campus to get lunch. They were basically prisoners from 9 to 5. Most times that she walked in the street, cars of men would stop and preposition her, offering $10, $20, $30... for her services, whatever they may be. This meant that I had to accompany her to the shop around 30 steps away, just to save her dignity.

It appeared that the local men soon realized that our apartment was comprised of foreigners, and the intensity of solicitation went up and soon turned violent. Sherry, a twenty-two-year-old fresh out of college, had wanted to experience living and working in the Middle East before settling into a career back in the States. Unlike Liz, she was not married and, after the first few times of getting prepositioned, she decided to wear the full *niqab*, which not only covered her body but her face as well. She figured that since Saudi women mainly wore this, she would not be bothered by the men as often.

One afternoon, on her way to the store, a car full of guys stopped and asked her to get in. She refused and started to run back the apartment. Arriving at the entrance, she screamed to Ibrahim behind the front desk to help her. He managed to close the door, allowing her just enough time to run into her apartment. The men pushed the door open and began to scream insults at Ibrahim, calling him a pig, slapping and spitting at him a few times. Sherry left Saudi soon after and vowed never to return.

During a play reading, a new couple could not find Brian and Sage's home. Liz volunteered to wave them inside, so she went out to the street—an isolated street. A young Saudi drove by, offering her 10 riyals, which worked out to be about two dollars and sixty cents USD. That was the last straw. After that, I did not let Liz out of my sight, except for the very, very rare occasion.

In Islam, it may be considered okay to lie or deceive an unbeliever. This is called *taqiya*. This mindset, coupled with a law system in Saudi that was favorable to Muslims, officially made non-Muslims second-tiered citizens.

For example, if a Saudi was involved in a car accident, the non-Muslim had to foot the bill, regardless if he was to blame or not. The thought behind this was: had the unbeliever not been there, the accident would not have taken place. Also, a non-Muslim's life was literally worth less than a Muslim's life. If you were involved in an accident and killed a Muslim, the blood money (yes, I said "blood money") used to appease the family was much more than if the deceased was non-Muslim. Saudi was biased towards Muslims in every facet of life.

The thing that struck me the most was that Saudi was the chief exporter of Islam all over the world, building Mosques in different countries and crying racial and religious discrimination; however, to practice another religion in Saudi was illegal and the fastest way to get your head removed from your body. It began to feel like the land of hypocrisy.

This attitude permeated on to the populous, thus allowing soliciting and sexual deviance against foreigners to go unchecked. In fact, the law stated that if a woman reported that she had been raped, she would need four, "upstanding", Muslim men to testify on her behalf. If there weren't four men to testify, then she did not scream out. (These multiple men would never have the sense to block her mouth, muffling her screams.) Thus, she must have enjoyed it. Therefore, logic dictates that if she enjoyed it, it was premarital sex, and she must either be stoned, whipped, or spend a lengthy sentence in prison.

The Saudi mentality had a habit of leaching onto the foreign Muslims. My desk partner, Juan, was an ex-Catholic, Muslim convert. While he did grow up in a conservative household, whereby the ideals of the man being the head of the household and the wife being subservient reigned supreme, Islam brought out new, exciting paths to explore for him.

After a week of small talk with Juan, he began talking about his wife and son that he left behind in Florida. He spoke passionately about his family and recalled the last time he saw them. He recounted a story that shall stick with me for the rest of my life...

His family went on a trip to Columbia, and at the airport on their way home, he got into a disagreement with his wife. After she did not want to relent, he grabbed her by the neck, took off his belt and struck her repeatedly. He felt that the public embarrassment would make her think twice about disobeying him in public. I was shocked into silence by what I was hearing.

He ended the story with a smirk, proudly believing he had taken the moral high ground. "The Quran commands a woman to obey her husband, and if she disrespects him, he is obliged to beat her with the strap."

Now, I will be the first to admit that the Bible, at times, had some questionable verses that were swept under the carpet come Sunday school time and forgotten by most. This was not so for Juan. I felt that he had a sociopathic personality and had used his religious views to further his own agenda. He felt emboldened.

With all that being said, Juan found out that as soon as he left to work in Saudi, his wife commenced divorce proceedings. This did not faze Juan. Being the smooth, handsome guy that he was, he always had a new woman on his arm at weekend parties. His aim was to have four wives in Saudi and continue with auditions till that day came. I always looked at his newest conquest with sadness, trying to make her run for the hills using telepathy. I wish I could have done more, but it wasn't my place.

Juan's bravado came to a grinding halt a few months after we first spoke. He and a few of his cronies went to the mall for dinner. The mall was full, and finding no seats at the single men section, they decided to sit at an open table at the family section. As time went by, Saudi did have the ability to lull one into a false sense of security, but they were shaken out of their stupor, literally. Unbeknownst to them, there was a Special Forces Unit sitting in the male section who had been observing them closely. The Special Forces Unit encircled them with military precision, grabbed them by the scruff of their necks and dragged them, kicking and screaming, out the mall.

They did, however, spare them the indignity of

roughing them up after they left the mall. They spent a few days in a holding cell, and they were released after a company rep bailed them out.

In Saudi, the only person(s) who was allowed bail out the incarcerated was the company reps. Since the company was the sponsor, they had to take full blame for the wrongdoings of the worker.

Our company was upset that this had shone a spotlight on them, and they left Juan and co. in jail for a couple of days to stew, as punishment.

We had the distinct displeasure of being invited to dinner with a fellow officemate, Jake. Jake was one of the guys who had moved to a private residence, along with Duncan and a few others. While we were all friends at the beginning, Jake had begun to ostracize his fellow roommates with his demand for silence at night, generally being cheap, wanting extra refrigerator space and his holier than thou ramblings.

One afternoon at work, he asked me out to dinner, and I figured that he needed someone to complain to. I wanted to be a good friend, yet, in the same breath, I was not looking forward to the dinner. I brought Liz to act as a buffer. Maybe he would be on his best behavior in the presence of a lady.

As soon as we sat down at the table, without missing a beat, he began to complain about anyone and everyone. Liz and I looked over the menus, nodding every so often. Jake told us that he was not hungry, so we went ahead and ordered.

Thinking that maybe a little food would slow his rambling, I told him that dinner was on us if he wanted a small bite. His eyes automatically lit up and ordered a starter, then a main dish and also a dessert—all of which were the most expensive items on the menu. In spite of all that, he never missed a second to complain about his fellow roommates.

When the bill came, he thanked us for dinner and promised us dessert at an ice-cream place close by. After we took care of the astronomical bill, Jake took us to the ice-cream parlor, bought one cup of ice-cream and handed each of us a spoon!

Liz and I looked at each other dumbfounded. I later found out that he owned apartments back in Canada and did not have any money problems. We never did have dinner again, even though he did offer to take me to McDonalds once.

He ended up shorting his roommates for rent a few times by claiming poverty. (He had a master's degree and with 10 years of experience, and he was earning more than most of us.) Finally, he was asked to leave the private residence after a five to zero vote in his disfavor.

The last conversation we had, he spoke about how his wife refused to hug him when he left to work in Saudi. While he thought that it was be-cause she was so distraught at him leaving, others thought it was because she could not stand him. I believed the latter.

My students had long past stopped showing up for class, but I still had a full and "busy" day. In the morning, I would go out for a full breakfast, and let it digest for hour or so, while catching up on the news, emails and such. Next, I would spend an hour in the gym, running on the treadmill, splashing in the hot tub and laying out in the sauna. Finally, a few of us would have lunch at another restaurant and meander back to the university.

By about that time in my day, my afternoon class would begin. We officially had to sit in the classroom for at least thirty minutes and could leave, if no one showed up. Usually I would sit around for 30 minutes, and then meet a few other teachers whose classrooms were also abandoned.

Since our classrooms had a large screen projector, we would watch movies, old boxing matches and an English sport, called cricket, which I had become quite fond of.

One afternoon, while getting ready to meet my colleagues for a Sugar Ray Leonard versus Thomas "The Hitman" Hearn's super fight, Ibrahim walking into my classroom. I was so surprised that I almost fell over. He told me that he was bored at home, and there really wasn't anything to do for a young person in Saudi. I welcomed him into the classroom and asked if he want to practice his English in conversion. He readily agreed, so I began asking how he was.

He responded, "I was sad. Abdul-Aziz died. He was drifting and rolled his car. No seat belt, so his arm got cut off and head was smashed. Three other people on road, dead."

Drifting was the latest craze, spreading amongst the bored youth in Saudi. Drifting involved taking bends at high speed and allowing the wheels to literally drift around a bend. It could be amazing if done in a controlled environment with no bystanders.

Unfortunately, drifting was done on the regular streets, frequently, even though it was officially banned and because there were no race tracks in Saudi. Fun of all shapes and sizes was banned. Going to our local grocer was akin to completing a gauntlet challenge. Young Saudis would speed by and take screeching corners at high speed. Many of the passengers would be hanging out the window, coaxing the driver on.

I felt terrible. A young life had been needlessly taken.

"But I got married, and I am happy now," continued Ibrahim.

My thoughts of an Arab Spring being brought about by young men not being able to marry came to mind, but it was quickly dashed when Ibrahim continued his story.

"I went to Morocco last month and had *nikah misyar*."

I looked at him and asked, "What is that, an ancient ritual?"

He answered, "I get married for three days, pay family for daughter and go home after."

I scratched my head. It sounded like legalized prostitution, but maybe I was missing something.

"Is there anything more? Does she come to see your family? Will you see her again?"

"No. Three days, hotel, *hallas* (finished). *Mafi mushkala* (no problem)."

Yep, it was exactly what I thought it was. I was shocked that Islam had found a theological decree to legalize prostitution. I found this baffling, especially when Saudis were a religious group of people that would drop everything to pray at the mosque. A taxi driver once stopped in the middle of the road and ran off to the closest mosque, leaving Liz and I looking baffled at each other at the back. People were ultra-religious.

This made me wonder about the power of religion. I once read that people are either good or bad, but it takes religion to make a good man, bad. While I did not necessarily agree with this, religion, like many other social practices, could be used to spread misinformation, such as the Jonestown cult tragedy. It seemed as if Ibrahim sipped the Kool-Aid of misinformation.

The problem seemed to rest with people and their interpretation of social practices to further their own agenda. While I pointed a finger at what I clearly saw as injustice, I realized that three fingers were pointing back at me. Was I a hypocrite? This made me introspective of myself and my practices.

Wanting to know even more about Saudi culture, we decided to go to a weekend-long festival called Janadriyah. Janadriyah was a celebration of traditional Saudi culture. We had fun petting Arabian horses, camels and an Arabian Oryx. We witnessed a traditional Saudi dance. We learned that while song and dance was frowned upon in Saudi, the traditional dance has its roots in being a war dance. Swords were waved around while, in camaraderie, the men held hands to cement the closeness of brothers in arms.

The traditional style of mud brick homes was on display, and one could even make their own brick and place it on a forming wall. We went in a traditional mud brick home and were served Arabian tea and dates.

The day turned out better than expected, until we had to go home. We had come with a company shuttle and were thankful that we were only ten minutes away from our home. Nothing is ever straightforward in Saudi, and our 10-minute trip turned into a one and half hour trip from hell.

One of the company managers came on our bus, just before we left, and demanded the driver take him home first. We literally drove within 2 minutes of our apartment before take a sharp turn onto a highway. We drove for another 40 minutes, halfway across the city, before we finally arrived at the villa owned by the company manager.

Another 40 minutes on some of the most dangerous roads in the world and with tempers fuming, we were finally dropped off at our apartment. If looks could kill, there would have been a bloodbath. Someone said under his breath, "What's the point of praying five times a day when one fails to understand the meaning of common courtesy?"

The best remedy for all this negativity? Play golf! The only person who showed interest in playing golf was Duncan, but truth be told, I would have went by myself if need be.

The next Friday, we met at the Intercontinental Hotel, ready for some action. The round of golf, including the golf club rental, came out to around $65. Money well spent. It was a basically a nine-hole golf course, but for the back nine, the tee boxes were moved to give the impression of playing a new hole. Behind the high walls, there was a metropolis. It was amazing what the architect had done to make the course seem as if you were in the middle of a meadow out in the country. The course was undulating with peaks and troughs, which made for an enjoyable experience.

From the get-go, we both realized that we would not return, because it was too expensive, but for today, we would take our time and enjoy every moment. All that was missing was a cold brewski in the desert sun, but even that was secondary to the fun of launching balls.

Back at school, Duncan relayed the fun we had,

and he ended his story by pointing to his hand, showing a big blister. "Well worth it!"

Someone from the back chirped in, "First world problems!"

Buoyed by the rejuvenating golf game, I enticed Liz to join me for a trip to Batha, the largest counterfeit goods market in Saudi Arabia. I had been warned by colleagues and students alike that Batha was a dangerous, lawless place with pick-pockets and unscrupulous vendors. I brushed off most of their concerns by jokingly saying that I lived in Detroit, and I was prepared for anything.

The miscreants in Batha must have had the day off, because we walked through many markets without any issues. I bought an Iraqi Dinar money note, with the picture Saddam Hussein on it, and a traditional Saudi curved dagger. (I later noticed that it was made in China.) I also purchased some knockoff Ray-Ban sunglasses and Levi jeans. All of those items were under $20.

The sunglasses didn't make the journey home. They fell on the ground, and the glass shattered into a hundred pieces. Too good to be true.

On the final leg of our journey, we walked into the goldsmith section. I had never seen so much gold in the same place. There were huge bars, chains and jewelry. Millions of dollars' worth of gold and no security guard in sight. I guessed the fear of losing a limb weighed heavily on any would-be thief.

We ended our trip by going to a traditional Filipino restaurant. I had the chicken adobo, and Liz had the squid in a sweet and sour sauce.

The squid was overcooked and resembled chewing on a leather belt. After trying in vain to break it down by mechanical digestion, she decided to move the squid down her throat, hoping chemical digestion did the rest of the work. The squid did not get that far. After swallowing, half of the tentacle remained in her mouth and the other half was halfway down her esophagus. I didn't notice this until she stood up and started trying to throw up while having her hands down her throat, trying to pull the tentacle out of her mouth.

A huge bodybuilder ran to Liz's aid, wanting to give her the Heimlich maneuver—all the while, she was trying to shoo him off with one hand. Liz eventually pulled the tentacle out of her mouth and summarily stormed out of the place. I was just about done with my food, so I thanked the big guy for trying to help, paid the bill and met Liz outside. Her face was as red as a tomato, and we both knew it was time to go back to our apartment.

In the middle of the night, I woke up with cold sweats and the feeling of a nuclear explosion in my gut area. For the next two days straight, I did not go to classes. I threw up and could not hold down any food or drink.

On the second evening, Liz called Noauf, and he took us to Kingdom Hospital within the hour. Thankfully, we didn't have to wait long at the hospital, and I was seen by a doctor within the first 15 minutes after arriving.

I was prescribed two different antibiotics and was asked to stay for an hour to get a saline drip to prevent dehydration. This was when my nightmare began.

A nurse came in the room to check my vitals and told us that she would be back in a few minutes with the drip. An hour later, just as we finally gave up and decided to just leave, she walked in with the saline bag. After literally five attempts at trying to find a vein, Liz impatiently asked her to find a doctor.

Ten minutes later, growing frustrated, Liz went to the hallway and cajoled a random nurse to insert the drip. Thankfully, this nurse did it in one go and quickly departed out the door. A few minutes later, we heard the call to prayer and looked at each other with horror. Would there be someone to remove the drip before the bag emptied. I had visions of getting an air bubble in my bloodstream.

I kept chanting, "I will not die in Saudi... I'm not gonna die in Saudi..."

As the saline bag began to empty, I started to get more frantic, sending Liz out into the hall to find a willing nurse. I began to contemplate removing the drip myself when the original nurse walked in, removed the needle from my arm and said, "You see? *Mafi mushkala.*"

CHAPTER 6
Letters from Liz, #2

Hello, everyone!

Sorry, it's taken so long for us to get back to you with an update. We've been working through a bit of culture shock while teaching in a foreign country, and now we have reached the end of the term. As we are nearing vacation, I thought I'd take some time to reflect on the things that I have experienced in the past 6 months.

Culture Shock #1: Show Me the Money

The attractive pay and benefits don't only attract English lecturers from around the globe, but also attract Saudi Arabia's own student population. You heard right: students actually get paid to attend "university". In fact, students get paid more than most unskilled laborers. This would include the immigrant population of custodians, shop attendants and baristas. With such a luxurious opportunity at Saudi students' fingertips, you'd think they'd be really keen on studying for their education, right?

This, brings me to...

Culture Shock #2: Are We Playing Hide and Seek?

Let me reminisce: My first week of teaching had arrived. I had my books, lesson plans and syllabus ready. I felt a mixture of excitement and anxiety as I prepared to meet my new class for the semester. I swung the door open and began a greeting, only to be welcomed to an empty classroom.

Okay, no problem. I set up my desk and loaded the smartboard and... waited... nothing. Not a single student. I began to get nervous. I checked to see if I was in the right classroom. I double-checked to see if I had the right time. All was sorted on my end, yet not a soul.

The next day was the same... In fact, the whole week was filled with empty desks. I spoke to my colleagues, and the same had happened to them. It seemed to be a campus-wide phenomenon...

I was just beginning to accept that I had a phantom class, when the following week, I had 4 students show up. The next day, a few more straggled in and so forth, until I reached a capacity of 16 young women.

That's when I learned my first lesson: Saudi time follows its own set of rules.

Culture Shock #3: Learning to Be as Flexible as a Gymnast

So, before I continue, let me do a quick recap. There I was in a classroom full of Saudi learners who had recently been paid a lump sum to attend class, yet incidentally were absent for the week. What was my first inclination, you might ask? As I looked out among these brightly lit faces, shining from the light of their mobile phones, I switched into dictator mode. I queued up my MS Power-Point, clearly stating that no phones were allowed in the classroom (picture of phone with red X over top of it.) Then, I informed them that their monthly payment depended on their attendance record. Good. I had laid down the law. I had made my expectations clear. I returned to my office feeling relieved and triumphant. Other colleagues also did the same. Good...

...and then one of my colleague's phone rang. It was the office. They had received multiple complaints from the students. They claimed that they couldn't understand her. They said that she had spoken ill of Islam. They said she called them names. None of that was true.

My colleague had taught for 15 years and had only received glowing reports from where she had worked before. She was known for being strict, but fair—a quality admired in the west. Either way, the Academic Affairs Office stated that the complaints were all her fault for not having a better "rapport" with her students. Thus, her job ended. Goodbye. Have a nice flight home. Which begs the question: Who is really in control of the classroom here?

After this happened, I quickly kissed my academic standards goodbye, because I was in Saudi. Not America. Not England. Not any western culture. The goal was to survive and keep my job for as long as possible. So, I learned to be flexible. I became very flexible, but I also learned how to keep my balance.

First, I made up a new item to the attendance list: "L" is for Late. My students didn't know that word; they only know "P" for present or "A" for absent. When they saw the "L", they asked me what it was, and I told them. They asked for the implications, and I just shrugged my shoulders and said, "I don't know. Be on time." Even though, in reality, there was no implication. However, they didn't know that, and they began coming to class and coming on time.

My superiors were happy because my students were attending class; my students were happy because they were getting paid; I was happy because at least the battle of getting them to come to class was won.

Next, I made up my own syllabus with participation grades and homework grades. I carefully recorded if they brought all their supplies to class and checked to see if they were actually doing the homework assigned to them. Doing homework was a chronic problem with the students. However, once they thought that it mattered, they started doing it. Er, well, actually most of them copied from the few that did it, but either way, at least they were glancing at some of the material. Since it really didn't count for anything, I didn't mind so much if they cheated (which is an avid part of their culture, known as "sharing answers"). Surprisingly (or not), those that did the homework did well on the tests, which actually did count for something.

Finally, I made friends with my superiors. That way, they could put a face with the name and hopefully think that I was a considerate, rational person that was friendly. This was important, because if a group of students decided they didn't like me and made up a complaint, my superiors would know that it was not in my character to act or behave in an uncouth manner.

Phewwww.... Job security set. "Pretend" grades and attendance carefully recorded. Academic integrity somewhat intact. Nice... and so, I continually attempted to cajole my students into learning, with its ups and downs, for the remainder of the semester.

Culture Shock #4: Coming to Terms

Finally, I came to terms with the realization that Saudi education is just for show. The best way I can describe it is this: it's like the No Child Left Behind Act on steroids, because after all the teachers meticulously submitted their grading and attendance, the Dean promptly rejected the grades and demanded a 95% pass rate (seriously).

It was easy to get frustrated, but I think it's better to just have a laugh. It's their country, and they can run it as dysfunctionally as they want. At the end of the day it doesn't really matter. After all, this "women's university" was really just a place for the girls to go and leave the confines of their house. Most of those women would never actually have a career. Most of them would get married, have 8-10 babies, and stay home all day with their hired Filipino nanny (or two) to look after the children.

The "university" was their time to leave behind their family, meet with their friends, text on their phones, maybe learn some English and Math, but mostly have some much-needed social interaction. In a society, where women are literally their husband's or father's property, and many don't leave the house without a male relative at their side, this was another "free" place for them—a place to shed their *niqab* and *abaya*, put on theatrical make-up and look as sexy as possible for their girlfriends. Love it or hate it, this is Saudi Arabia.

<u>Current Disposition</u>

So now, here we are, mandated to continue coming into work, even though all the grades were entered and there are no more classes left to teach. Lately, I've been occupying myself with a British sitcom, *Gavin and Stacey.* The whole office has really been enjoying it. Tomorrow, I'm going to learn to play the game Cribbage!

Alex and I have also been becoming more active. Alex joined a gym, and I joined the Triathletes Club. I've been focusing on swimming twice a week for an hour at a time and have been distancing around 2,000 meters a session. I'm feeling more fit than I did in Michigan. I've done 3 biathlons so far and plan to do my next one this Friday —a 500-meter swim followed by a 3km run.

It's been really fun. Alex comes to watch, and we all have breakfast together afterward. It's been a great way to meet some new people that have other professions in Saudi (nurses, business men, etc.) Plus, it's nice to get out of the apartment and not be draped head to toe in sun absorbing black fabric. The best part?! I can wear a normal one-piece bathing suit. Since no Saudis are allowed to join the triathlete club, I can avoid wearing the unfashionable modest swimwear.

Another thing we've been occupying ourselves with on the weekend is "The Hash." The Hash is basically a name for a club that likes to walk and run outside in the desert. It's a huge weekly event that draws anywhere from 150-200 people. Everyone is foreign, and as you probably guessed, no abayas are necessary! The Hash is my only chance to wear shorts outside. It's really fun, and it's amazing to see the effects of wind and water erosion on what was once an oasis.

It definitely is warming up these days, with evening temperatures in the high 30's (90's) and the sunny days in the late 40's (110+). We are definitely looking forward to vacation. In fact, vacation is just around the corner! We are leaving for vacation in a week's time to relax in the mild winter weather of South Africa for a month. However, the good news doesn't end there. We will also be gracing Michigan's shores with our presence sometime mid-July. We look forward to visiting with all of you then and catching up on the local news.

Thank you for your prayers. We've had a relatively smooth transition here. We also haven't had a traffic accident since the last time I wrote to you (about 4 months ago). Yippee!

Some things we would like to ask you to pray about in the meantime:

1. We are going on vacation in 7 days, but we haven't booked a ticket because our company still has our passports. The problem is that we are under a "work visit visa", which needs to be renewed every 90 days. Both of our passports were due to expire May 24, and we turned ours in early, hoping we could get a turnaround in the next few weeks. Three weeks have come and gone and still no passports. It's very hard to plan for a vacation and pack, and it's impossible to send money into our bank accounts without a passport. Please pray that both of ours will arrive on time for us to fly out and see Alex's family.

2. Please continue to pray for safety on the roads. It seems like as things are heating up tem-

perature-wise in the desert, people are getting even more reckless with their vehicles. It's especially dangerous to walk outside amongst the crazy adolescent boys that like to drift. A sad fact: About every week a student at King Saud University will die due to drifting accidents. I guess this is what happens when fuel is cheap, and boys have too much time on their hands.

Thanks for your prayers. We are looking forward to seeing you all soon!

Peace,
Liz

CHAPTER 7
The Last Estraha

Saudi Arabia has been, and continues to be, the number one violator of human rights, along with Iran, North Korea, and a few other countries. While it is a highly conservative country, because of our job and citizenship, we were sheltered from and failed to see many of the human rights violations. We began to get a false sense of security and became relaxed, and we became emboldened with our weekend extracurricular activities.

Walking around the city in the evening became monotonous, and we grew tired of trying out new restaurants and getting sick from them. I'm not sure if it was the heat causing the food to go bad or just a lack of hygiene, but we would often get a 24-hour stomach flu. Since I was on acid reducers, I tended to be sicker with stomach ailments longer than Liz.

Growing tired of this, we generally stuck to our tried-and-tested places to eat, but this was also becoming boring. We spent a night wandering Riyadh's pedestrian friendly Tahlia Street, which was close to the skyscraper, Faisaliah Tower. After an Indian dinner at a great restaurant called Copper Chandi and having had the best butter chicken and korma we had ever eaten to date, we walked off our food and happened upon the hotel district.

We wandered around till we saw a sign outside a Holiday Inn, advertising a room, including the breakfast and lunch buffet. We decided to splurge. Being in the hotel room felt like a break from Saudi, which was beginning to wear us down.

We had tried many different ways of getting our minds off the fact that we were in one of the most restrictive countries in the world. Compounds were fun but a nightmare to get into, and food and drinks were expensive. We did have the pleasure of seeing a play. That may not sound profound, but it was worth noting that plays were banned in Saudi and therefore had to be performed in a guarded compound performed by foreigners. The story was a simple one of love lost and reunited, and we wondered if we would share the same feeling with Saudi. South Korea had a special place in our hearts as we met there, but only time would tell if we would share that feeling with Saudi Arabia.

It was around this time that a few of our close-knit friends began holding Friday night gatherings at *estrahas*. An *estraha* was a type of resort in a country that was devoid of resorts. It was by no means a typical resort, but one done Saudi-style.

The building was generally enclosed with a high wall and a steel door to keep prying eyes at bay.

Once you walked through the door, there were usually a small grassed area, where you could congregate with a grill and a pool. The pool was sometimes enclosed by a roof. There was one or two small houses on the property used for parties or segregating the sexes. It was just a place to let loose and pretend that you were in a normal country with normal rules. Some brought wine, including myself, food and parlor games. For many, just relaxing in the pool became akin to a religious experience.

The *estraha* entrance was a large, steel door with a peephole, reminiscent of a speakeasy. The first few weeks, we all tried to draw as little attention as possible, coming fully dressed, not forgetting for a moment where we were, and moving through the steel door with speed as not to put any spotlight on what was going on behind closed doors.

These gatherings happened fortnightly, and at first, it was a small bunch of mature people having a good time but never forgetting where we were. Over the next couple of weeks, the group of people started to increase, becoming ever-younger, with more energy and carefree, nonchalant attitudes.

On the night of our last *estraha*, this all came to a head. We were celebrating the birthday of a close friend, who was quite popular in his own right. Within a week of being in Saudi, he had networked himself into different professional groups, and within a month, he had created a company employing teachers. He had rented out the *estraha* in the past, but for his birthday, he had chosen a newer, larger one, quite a distance away from where we lived, on the outskirts of the city, close to the empty desert.

We were a bit hesitant to go, since we knew it would be the largest one yet, but the idea of the party being in an isolated place kept our fears at bay. We invited and shared a taxi with Amy, an American friend of Liz's, to save some cash.

When our taxi dropped us off at the *estraha*, while on the outskirts of the city, the area was suburban with new developments all around—not as isolated as we thought. The music was noticeably louder when we got out of the taxi. The door was made of steel, and knocking on it created a stentorian boom.

As like our previous parties at *estrahas*, the person manning the door opened a peephole to see who was at the door, and recognizing us, he opened the door immediately.

This property seemed smaller inside, and with the high walls, there was only one way in or out. The yard had a pool, and at the far end of the lawn was a small, double-story house. Inside the house, there was a DJ playing pop music and large, moonshine drink dispensers taking up the rest of the dining room.

Liz and I went upstairs, and both of us stripped down to our bathing suits. Since no one had gone in the pool yet, we decided to break the ice. The water was cool and refreshing. Soon, a few more people came in, and we played a few games of Marco Polo.

Afterwards, the desert air dried us off quickly, and with two glasses of wine in hand, we found our friends. The evening was going great. However, every so often, the big steel door would open, and more people would flood in.

The door opening protocol began to suffer as the night wore on. The door would be open for extended periods of time, with Saudis on the street peering in. Ladies arrived in miniskirts and swimwear, forgetting which country they currently resided in.

Against my better judgment, I brushed off my ill feelings, but after a while, I felt it was getting close to leaving time. The party was getting out of control, and the moonshine was not helping matters.

All of a sudden, there was a loud booming noise emanating from the front door of the complex. I looked around, and with the loud music and happy drunkenness, nobody seemed to take notice. I looked back at the door, and after a final boom, the door swung open violently. On the other side of the door were men with long beards and white *thobes*, wielding a battering-ram. Everyone looked dumbstruck, but before most could react, an army of men stormed the complex.

A light bulb went off in my head, and I realized it was the religious police: the *Mutaween*. I felt like I was in a dream sequence of a movie. The air seemed foggy, and everyone moved in slow motion. All around me people were running and screaming and getting hit with camel prods.

Standing in the center of the complex, everything appeared to happen around me, without actually getting to me. The flight or fright cognition kicked in, and without thinking, I began to walk towards the complex door.

The *Mutaween*, hellbent on their mission at hand, rushed into all areas of the complex including the house, but ignored me. I reached the outside of the estraha and stood on the road, looking around. Many of the men had walked out as well without much resistance, and after seeing the *Mutaween* try to grab a couple trying to leave, something in my mind clicked. They were letting the men leave but not the women. Liz!

In my dazed flight out of the complex, I had totally lost track of Liz. I heard a loud scream that sounded familiar. I ran back into the complex and straight into the house. People were afraid and cowering in corners, while the *Mutaween* tussled with a couple of guys who were refusing to go quietly.

I looked around quickly, and not seeing Liz, I ran out and checked the back of the house. Liz was grouped together with Ben, Vergil and a couple of other ladies. Ben was trying to boost the ladies over the wall while Vergil kept watch. I grabbed Liz by the hand and went inside the garden shed to hide. There was one other person inside, so it made for a tight fit. Almost hyperventilating, we realized that we could not stay in there for long. The only problem was that Liz's *abaya* was in the house, on the top floor, and the house was swarming with *Mutaween*. We needed to make a decision quickly.

"If we leave this place without my *abaya*, we will be pulled over by the police! It's illegal! What are we going to do?" said Liz frantically.

I did not have an answer, but I knew that we could not stay where we were. While the adrenaline was pumping, we pushed open the door of the shed and jogged towards the entrance of the *estraha*.

While jogging, Liz grabbed two towels on the floor to accompany the t-shirt and tank top already clutched in her right hand. We got to the entrance, and we were completely blocked by the *Mutaween*. Bravado won over and I took Liz by the hand like a steel vice and pushed through the *Mutaween*. They hit us with a range of items, including prayer beads, camel prods and their bare hands. Pulling ourselves through the group at the entrance, they began to spit at us and shout out obscenities. We finally managed to find ourselves on the road and discovered that it was cordoned off with the *Mutaween's* vehicles. We managed to shimmy through the multitude of vehicles, witnessing fistfights between some men at the party and the *Mutaween*. This was the distraction we needed, and we ran to the end of the street.

We stood on the corner of the street, panting for breath and noticed, for the first time, that Liz was in her bikini. She quickly wrapped one towel around her head and the other around her waist. *Abayas* in Saudi had to be black, but the towels were white. Realizing this, we decided to get to a main street to hail a taxi. It was dangerous, but it was our best move.

As we walked briskly out of the area, Saudis drove up to us, screaming for us to get in their vehicle so that they could help us by taking us to an embassy. We almost relented, but by our better judgment, we kept walking without acknowledging their presence.

Something that Sath said came to mind. He mentioned that every Saudi was considered a *Mutaween*. Big brother was always watching.

Most drove off after noticing that we had no interest in their offer. Later on, we found out the a few people who took their offer were driven to a police station and not an embassy. They were summarily incarcerated.

After walking a few hundred yards, a car screeched next to us with people we recognized from the party. Screaming at us to get in, while opening the car door, Liz and I dove into the car.

The wheels quickly spun into action, and we were off at a high speed.

One of the Saudis that had offered us a ride earlier chased after the car, shining a large spotlight on us. The driver began to freak out and made a couple of sharp turns in a suburban maze. When it seemed as if we had lost our assailant, the driver told us to exit the vehicle so that he could throw them off our trail. The selfless driver did get followed again, and upon reaching his home, was dragged out of his vehicle and put in handcuffs.

We jumped out the car and split up into groups, hoping to confuse any would be pursuers. Joining us was a 22-year-old Canadian Ethiopian lady, named Kadisha, who looked like she had seen a ghost. We quickly tried to get as far away as we could, but after just a few yards, cars came speeding along the road and drove past us. Feeling relieved for a moment, we continued to walk, but all of a sudden, one of the cars slammed on their brakes and put its reverse lights on. We opened the gate of the closest yard and shuffled into an apartment complex. While hiding behind the wall of apartment complex, Liz took the moment to reevaluate her wardrobe. She noticed she had an oversized forest green t-shirt she put over her bikini top, a black tank top she put over her hair and used the remained towels to cover her waist and knees. Knowing we couldn't remain in a strangers yard behind their fence we exited the gate climbed a few steps and walked along the edge of the wall attempting to lose our pursuers.

After what seemed like an eternity (but was closer to 5 minutes), we walked out of the complex hoping to find a main road. The road appeared to be empty. Retracing our steps, Kadisha told us that she remembered seeing a busy road a few blocks back, while we had been couriered at a high speed earlier. We began heading in that direction, but out of the corner of my eye, I saw a Saudi standing at the front gate, pretending to open a lock but keeping his eyes trained on us. The hairs at the back of my neck stood up, and something did not feel right. The gusting hot desert air did nothing to alleviate my suspicions. The wind had begun to pick up dust from the floor. Shielding my eyes from sand, I noticed the Saudi at the gate of a yard gesturing to someone in a car who had just arrived at the gate. The Saudi outside the car pointed in our direction and quickly climbed in the car. The car sped towards us and then came to a screeching halt. The car was the same car with the spotlight attached to the side mirror that had followed us earlier.

"*Maffi mushala*, no problem, we take you to embassy! Come! Come!" They chanted this a few times. Noticing that we were ignoring them, they sped off.

At this point, our adrenaline was pumping through our veins, and we doubled up on our pace to reach the main road. When we got to the main road, the two ladies waited in the shadows as not to attract attention. I became conscious of the fact that I was wearing swimming trunks that were above my knee. In Saudi, men were encouraged to wear pants that were below the knee. During the summer, men not wanting to wear the *thobe* would often be seen with peddle pusher pants.

I stood out by the main road, for the longest fifteen minutes of my life, and not a single taxi came by. Feeling a little anxious from the idea of being sitting targets, we decided to walk to a busier intersection about a hundred yards down the road. As we got to the corner, a policeman directing traffic spotted us and began to walk in our direction. I had my hand out trying to hail a passing taxi, but the car with the spotlight stopped in front of us, shined their light directly on us and screamed in Arabic at the top of their voices, trying to wave the policeman in our direction.

This was becoming a spectacle, and people were beginning to stop and look in our direction. The intersection was next to a soccer stadium, and even in the middle of the night, a game was going on. I had chosen the worst possible place to be.

Liz was praying to Jesus. Kadisha was praying to Allah. I was standing there, staring at the policeman quickly approaching me. Fear enveloped me, and I began to wonder if everything that we had done to avoid capture was all for naught.

As the policeman approached me, the two

Saudis got out of their vehicle and continued to scream in Arabic at the top of their lungs. The policeman looked at them and put his finger on his lips, indicating that they should stop talking. He said a few things that the girls and I couldn't understand, and the men started screaming again, pointing at us. The policeman talked again, pointing at their car. They got back into their car, clearly disgruntled and drove away. I held my breath, and the policeman came up to me, looking at Liz wrapped in towels and Kadisha next to her, clearly knowing what was going on.

"*Salam Alaykom!*" exclaimed the policeman.

"*Alaykom Salam*," I replied.

"You from America?"

"Yes," I answered, still uncertain of what fate awaited us.

"What are you doing out this late?"

"We had some dinner, and now we are looking for a taxi. All we want to do is go home."

Dumbfounded, we watched as the police officer hailed us a taxi, with an Afghani driver, clearly a bit confused, and just like that, the police officer sent us off... with Liz in a t-shirt, a black tank top covering her hair, and a towel wrapped around her waist and another around her knees and me in a bathing suit.

We had found a way out of the endless night, the endless maze. Perhaps the divine intervened, or the police officer's indifference prevailed. So, thank you Jesus, Allah and the subpar, Saudi, work ethic, you made a way of escape where there was none, and for that, we were truly thankful.

"*Masalaama*," the policeman said, waving us into the taxi.

We didn't need to be told twice and swiftly got into the taxi. We told the taxi driver our destination, and we all huffed a collective sigh of relief.

Once we arrived back at our apartment, we swapped stories of our harrowing escape, and after Kadisha's brother came to pick her up, we finally were able to get some much-needed rest.

Two hours later, Liz stirred me awake, asking if I had seen Amy throughout the whole affair. I had not, so Liz called her phone, and it went straight to voicemail. I texted Ben and Vergil, and within a few minutes, I was told that all the people that were captured at the party were loaded up into SUV's and hauled to the desert. We didn't get much additional information, except to "call the American Embassy".

Liz frantically called the embassy, explaining what had transpired, but she was told that they could only look into the matter in the morning. After an uneasy couple hours of sleep, Liz called the embassy in the morning, and she was told that they would try to look into the matter.

At around 11am, Liz called again, asking if they had any updates on the situation. She was politely told that they were still looking into the matter and would call her if there was any change. Amy's phone still went straight to voicemail, and Liz was beginning to get frantic.

"She came with us! We had a duty to protect her!" Liz burst out, as she paced around the apartment.

She was right. We had arrived with Amy, and I felt terrible that we didn't know where she was.

At 5pm, Amy called Liz, informing her that she had been in prison, but the company had come to get them out. Amy was in prison less than 24 hours, but the experience had forever changed her life. Ben and Vergil texted a short while later telling me that they were released from prison as well and were on their way back to the apartment. Both asked me to chill some wine as they needed a couple of mugs of wine to ease their nerves.

Amy, Vergil and Ben convened in our apartment that evening, each being given a bottle of wine to take the edge off. After a few glasses of wine, Amy began to talk first.

"It all happened so fast. I was having a shower in my bikini, then I heard screaming in the room. A bearded man, which I later realized was a *Mutaween* operative, banged on the shower door. I open the door, and his eyes lit up. He tried to put his hands down my bikini bottoms, and I started screaming. Alarmed, the *Mutaween*, pulled back for just a second, and that was enough time for me to run out the shower. There were more *Mutaween* in the room, but there were also some men from the party, so I felt safe for a bit. I quickly put on my *abaya*, saw yours on the bed and wondered how you would leave without it."

Liz began to cry then and shared with us for the first time that when the complex was first raided, a Mutaween had tried to grope her, as well, but she screamed at the top of her lungs, and he moved on to someone else. At that moment, I felt as though I had failed to protect Liz, and I was ashamed.

Amy continued, "The *Mutaween* told the men they could leave. They only wanted the ladies. The men in the house knew their intentions and refused to go. Bless their hearts. I am forever grateful to those brave men. Next, we were loaded up into their SUV's and carted off to the desert. Everyone was confused. Why were we going to the desert? A few people were tossed out of the SUV and told to sit on the ground. A few of the old *Mutaween* then proceeded to walk off to a few yards and started to talk amongst themselves. A few voices were raised, then came frantic hand gestures and then silence.

"They finished off their cigarettes and flicked them on the group that sat on the desert sands. Some stormed into their vehicles and sulked, while the others put down a carpet on the floor and sat around and talked quietly amongst themselves.

"After an hour, they made us all get back in the SUV's and drove for about 30 minutes. The ladies were dropped off at women's prison, while the men were taken to their respective jail. We were so scared, but we had no idea of the true horrors that awaited. Amy shuddered reliving that night.

"We were placed in a jam-packed holding cell that resembled limbo... and it was for some. There were eight women from the party in total, and we found a corner and huddled together. Once I had a moment to calm myself and acclimate, I took a look around the holding cell and was shocked, dumbfounded, and horrified. Only the coldest, most inhumane people would cause what I witnessed in that cell.

"The holding cell was filled with young ladies, most Filipino. Some were at different stages of pregnancy, and others who did not have guardians in Saudi, held their newborn babies. Some ladies had gone insane and were throwing their feces at the ceiling. This was a room of injustice and desperation. A Filipino lady with a young baby in her arms saw that some of us were crying and came over to comfort us. She introduced herself as Angel.

"She said, 'Don't worry. You are from countries that Saudi respects and has strong embassies. You will get out soon. Every week, we have a group of ladies from western countries come to jail, and they always leave within a week.'

"Without thinking, I blurted out, 'You are in jail with a baby. These people are monsters. What happened...?'

"Angel looked at us and started her story: 'Like most of the ladies here, I came to Saudi to work as a housemaid. As soon as I got to the house of my employer, he took my passport. I didn't realize it then, but I was trapped. Not long after that, first the boss then his teen son would rape me. Eventually, I fell pregnant, and when I started to show, the boss called the *Mutaween* and told them that I am unmarried and pregnant. This is against the law, so I was taken to this holding cell, and I have been here for eight months.

'They don't allow me to speak with my embassy, and even if I could, I'm not sure what they can do. I miss my home and family. Please contact my embassy. They can contact my parents, and they can take care of my baby.'

Just as Angel said, we were released in the morning. That night changed my life forever. I hope to put a spotlight on these gross human rights violations being perpetrated in Saudi. The embassy is closed over the weekend, but I plan to take off tomorrow and go to the Philippines Embassy. They need to know, and I owe it to Angel and all those ladies who have been treated in the most inhumane manner. Their only crime is that they are victims without a voice."

Looking around the room, we were all shocked, and some were in tears at hearing this injustice.

After our guests left, Liz and I sat down quietly, knowing what was in each other's hearts and minds. We had forsaken and sold our personal liberties and rights for oil money. In doing so, we felt we did our bit to legitimize a rogue state. That all ended that very moment. We packed our bags and hastily sold off a few of our possessions that couldn't make it on the plane to our apartment friends. I gave Ben and Vergil a 20-liter container of my soon-to-be fermented wine and decided to hold off leaving until we got our salary envelopes of cash the next day. We had enough.

Since the status of most of the teachers was in legal limbo and a grey area, we could not open bank accounts. Overseas transfers were done under the table by a few select banks on behalf of our company. Since we could not have direct pay, we had to sit in a large lecture room to receive our money. A group of accountants sat in the front and called our names individually. With a staff of 300 plus employees, this could take forever, depending on when your name was called. When you received your pay, it was in a thick envelope. Most teachers did not trust the company and counted out their money right there on the spot. More often than not, it was correct, but a few times it wasn't, so guys made a big scene. It was known that if your payout was short, it would take a few months to correct it. The distribution of pay took a weird turn. I guess the motto in Saudi was if it isn't broke, try and break it.

Someone in management had the bright idea to take the handing out of pay from the air-conditioned comfort of the lecture theatre and make the teachers stand in a line, in which the majority of the people standing were outside in the un-forgiving desert sun. We stood around for almost an hour with the line barely moving, and then the most unlikely of things occurred: It started to rain. Chaos ensued. Teachers stormed the small room that was holding the accountants, causing them to gather their gear and run for the hills. All the while, I stood in the rain, hoping that it would wash away my sins and then wondering when I would be paid, thanking my lucky stars that we had not yet purchased plane tickets. Saudi had conspired to keep us there against our will.

Most of us didn't get paid that day, and we received a mass email apologizing for what had transpired. The powers that be decided to go back to the original way of handing out our pay checks. The next day, the rest of us received our checks during our lunch break. After lunch, I walked in my next class. Unsurprisingly, it was empty. I threw my marker at the wall in silent protest, walked out the entrance of the building, hailed a cab to our apartment and booked our tickets for that very night.

Noauf graciously drove us to the airport and re-ported with much sadness that he was still unable to find a job in the medical field. After a few heart-felt goodbyes from friends that I would cherish for the rest of my life, we departed the hell on Earth known as the Magical Kingdom of Saudi Arabia, but not without incident.

We wondered if we were legally bound to the

country until released by our company, but remembering all the midnight runs of the past, we didn't fixate on it. While standing in line, butterflies were in our stomachs and excitement abounded.

I felt a tap my shoulder. Turning around, I noticed that it was someone that I had seen before at the campus but had never spoke, too. I would often see him sitting at the table of hardliners who came across as holier than thou, never interacting with anyone. I found it strange that he was speaking to me now.

"Hey, I remember seeing you on campus. You guys leaving?"

"My wife's father died," I blurted out the lie without hesitation, knowing that was a safe reason for leaving and not dancing on anyone living's grave, since Liz's father had died ten years earlier.

He offered his sympathies and cut straight to the chase. "I have a couple of bottles of holy water from Medina, and they only allow one per customer. Could you check this in for me?"

Air Travel Etiquette 101: never check in items for someone else. If anything is wrong with it, you are liable.

I shook my head and explained, "I would like to help you, but I don't feel comfortable, since it is against the law..." He stormed off, cursing me under his breath, and he went to try and convince someone else in line.

Liz and I checked in our bags, and we breathed sighs of relief. Until that very moment, I didn't realize how truly grateful I was for the blessing to make the choice to leave when so many others were forced to stay—some literally in prison and some figuratively imprisoned under Saudi laws.

I tried to be appreciative for the lessons that I learned during our year in Saudi, but all I could think of was how thankful I was to get the hell out, vowing never to return.

As we boarded the plane, neither Liz nor I looked back. We were free.

REFERENCES & RESOURCES

Tripp H & North P. (2003). Culture Shock Saudi Arabia

Cover Photo by Tariq Almutlaq

ABOUT THE AUTHORS

Alex and Liz Fletcher have lived and worked in Africa, South Korea and Saudi Arabia, and they now reside in the Michigan. Alex currently teaches English at the college level and has a master's degree in English Education. Liz went back to school, and she now works in the medical field. In their spare time, they enjoy hiking and camping in national parks with their two kids.

Made in the USA
Middletown, DE
29 June 2019